National Assessment Institute

HANDBOOK FOR SAFE
FOOD SERVICE MANAGEMENT

SECOND EDITION

Prentice Hall
Upper Saddle River, New Jersey 07458

Library of Congress Cataloging-in-Publication Data

Handbook for safe food service management / National Assessment
  Institute. — 2nd ed.
     p.   cm.
  Includes index.
  ISBN 0-13-236118-3 (pbk.)
   1. Food service—Sanitation. 2. Food service—Safety measures.
 I. National Assessment Institute.
 TX911.3.S3H36   1998
 363.72'96—dc21   97-10103
                                    CIP

Author: *National Assessment Institute*
Revision Coordinators: *Bryn Knight and Dr. Mark Tamplin*
Production Editor: *Adele M. Kupchik*
Managing Editor: *Mary Carnis*
Acquisitions Editor: *Neil Marquardt*
Director of Manufacturing and Production: *Bruce Johnson*
Manufacturing Buyer: *Ed O'Dougherty*
Editorial Assistant: *Rose Mary Florio*
Marketing Manager: *Frank Mortimer, Jr.*
Formatting/Page makeup: *Bryn Knight/ComCom, an R.R. Donnelley & Sons Company*
Printer/Cover Printer/Binder: *R.R. Donnelley & Sons, Crawfordsville, IN*
Cover Design: *Bruce Kenselaar*
Cover Photo: *Richard Embery*

© 1998, 1994 by Prentice-Hall, Inc.
Simon & Schuster/A Viacom Company
Upper Saddle River, New Jersey 07458

Printed in the United States of America

10 9 8 7 6 5 4 3 2 1

ISBN 0-13-236118-3

Prentice-Hall International (UK) Limited, *London*
Prentice-Hall of Australia Pty. Limited, *Sydney*
Prentice-Hall Canada Inc., *Toronto*
Prentice-Hall Hispanoamericana, S.A., *Mexico*
Prentice-Hall of India Private Limited, *New Delhi*
Prentice-Hall of Japan, Inc., *Tokyo*
Simon & Schuster Asia Pte. Ltd., *Singapore*
Editora-Prentice-Hall do Brasil, Ltda., *Rio de Janeiro*

Contents

Preface

National Assessment Institute

National Assessment Institute (NAI) is a leader in providing examination services, and prides itself in setting standards of excellence for professional licensure and certification. NAI operates nationwide, in all 50 states, and services more than 130 city, county, state, and national licensing authorities. Its continued leadership in this field paves the way for quality examinations that are credible and reliable.

National Certified Professional Food Manager Certification

The National Assessment Institute is dedicated to the National Certified Professional Food Manager program. Our goal is to provide a total learning system to regulators, the food service industry, and individuals with both up-to-date, comprehensive training materials and a nationally recognized examination that is valid, legally defensive, and meets individual and collective needs. NAI recognizes that a national food program is a natural extension of, or a component of, the food service industry; therefore, consistency and cooperation with regulatory organizations, industry groups, and individual candidates are necessary to achieve success.

The National Certified Professional Food Manager (CPFM) certification is a professional stamp of approval for individuals working in the food service industry. In some states and municipalities, this type of certification is required by law. However, many food service employees voluntarily seek certification to enhance their credentials and attain additional respect in their field. Certification not only allows them to achieve the goal of protecting the public health, but also serves to increase their rate of professional growth.

Two steps are required to achieve this professional goal. First, candidates must complete the curriculum of the Safe Food Service Management program. Second, they must pass the National Certified Professional Food Manager (CPFM) examination.

Candidate Training

Training is covered in the textbook *Handbook for Safe Food Service Management*. The Handbook provides the basic educational components needed to become a Certified Professional Food Manager.

Numerous registered sanitarians and educators in the field reviewed and approved the *Handbook for Safe Food Service Management*. All course materials were reviewed by a professional linguist to assure clarity. The Handbook is written from a "need-to-know" viewpoint, which makes access to vital information easy.

Today's customer demands a safe and responsible approach to food service and sanitation. The Hazard Analysis Critical Control Points (HACCP) system is introduced in an easy-to-read, logical sequence. NAI's learning system covers the key elements of safe food handling and storage.

Instructional Component

Current criteria for NAI instructor certification require that first, applicants meet the qualifications required by the state or jurisdiction in which they will be teaching, and second, that they have sufficient experience in the field of food management.

The Instructional Program has been developed as a 15-hour course. If a jurisdiction requires a different number of hours of course instruction, the national CPFM program can be expanded or contracted to meet the required hours. One of the strengths of the national CPFM program is its flexibility. It can be customized to meet specific client, state health agency, or jurisdictional requirements.

In those states where there is a course requirement for food managers, candidates are not deemed eligible to take the examination until proof of eligibility is received. In most cases, the instructor is also a certified NAI proctor.

If you contact NAI, we will notify you of the closest instructor in your area. In most cases, the examination will be held at the institution where you take your course of study.

Course Completion

For information regarding a course available in your area, call National Assessment Institute at (800) 200-4261. Or you can write us at:

National Assessment Institute
600 Cleveland Street, Suite 1000,
Clearwater, FL 34615
Telephone: (813) 449-8525 Fax: (813) 461-2746

The Certified Professional Food Manager Examination

Different locations around the country have specific requirements regarding their Food Manager Certification examinations. National Assessment Institute develops the appropriate certification and/or licensure examination for each location that varies from the national norm.

The examination is referenced to the *Handbook for Safe Food Service Management*. Two new forms of the examination will be developed to coincide with the release of the second edition of the Handbook. The examination is designed to measure the minimum knowledge, skills, and abilities for entry level competency, to protect the public.

There are eight unique forms of the examination. All forms contain 80 questions with a one-hour time limit. It can easily be finished in that time period. The content of the National CPFM examination is based on the Accreditation Study Committee, Council II, Conference for Food Protection's recommended criteria for the food manager's responsibilities.

Currently, successful completion of an examination is required in some states but not in others. Some areas of the country require both the completion of a course of study with a specified number of educational hours and a passing score on the examination. For areas that require only the examination, the CPFM examination may be approved. Check with local authorities.

Preparation for the Examination

In order to be relaxed and confident by the time you take the examination, study and prepare a little each day. This helps you to better absorb the material and eliminates last-minute cramming.

Leave for the test center in plenty of time. A stressful drive through heavy traffic can ruin your concentration.

Once inside the examination room, relax and take your time. You have more than enough time to carefully read and answer all of the examination questions.

Rules of conduct during the examination require that you do not talk to other candidates. Mobile telephones or beepers are not allowed in the examination room. No smoking is allowed in the room. If you do not follow the rules, you may be asked to leave before completing your examination, and lose the fee.

Special Needs

Candidates with special needs will be taken care of at the test sites. Arrangements can be made for the visually and hearing impaired. If English or Spanish is not your primary language, contact NAI for special arrangements.

Those with physical handicaps, as well as those with learning disabilities, will find that help is available simply by contacting NAI. We can handle any special requirements.

Taking the Examination

All of the questions are multiple choice with only one correct answer. There are four different choices and you are to choose only one.

* Make sure that only one choice for each question is marked on your answer sheet.

* Answer all of the questions.

* There is no penalty for guessing.

* Take your time.

* You will have ample time to complete the examination.

The examination has four main topic areas:

* Food

* Service facilities

* Sanitary habits for food handlers

* Management

Examples of subject areas included in the examination are:

* Applying the HACCP system for food safety

* Receiving and inspecting food and supplies

* Safe storage of food and supplies

* Food contamination

* Preparing and serving safe foods

* Storage of leftovers or pre-prepared foods

* Personal hygiene practices

* Equipment and utensils

- Cleaning and sanitizing food contact surfaces
- Using dishwashing machines
- Using and storing poisonous or toxic materials
- Avoiding accidents and injuries

Notification of Examination Results

Each candidate who takes the national CPFM examination receives a score report or certification card. Successful candidates receive a wallet-size certification card. Depending on when we receive your answer sheets, NAI will send either you or your instructor notice of examination results. If you do not pass your examination, you will be given the opportunity to be reexamined at a later date. An additional fee will be charged.

Additional Products Available

- A wall certificate suitable for hanging in your home or place of work.

- A beautifully crafted cloisonne lapel pin featuring the Certified Professional Food Manager's logo.

- A window emblem displaying the national CPFM logo. This emblem may be placed in your vehicle or at your place of employment.

- A colorful T-shirt with the national CPFM emblem.

National Registry

All candidates are listed in a National Registry. The registry is designed to capture information and generate statistics not only for the whole but also on specific jurisdictions or corporations. This makes it very convenient for clients to keep track of the pass and fail rates within their jurisdiction, and it also allows NAI to look at how well the examination performs compared to other jurisdictions. We watch these statistics closely to ensure that the validity and integrity of the program remain intact.

MAKE THE SMART CHOICE —
BECOME A RESPECTED CERTIFIED PROFESSIONAL FOOD MANAGER

Acknowledgment

This book is the culmination of over two years of research, investigation, analysis, and rewrites of the original text. A strong debt of gratitude is owed by National Assessment Institute to Bryn Knight for her dedication and perseverance in taking this text from its initial 1994 edition to this revised 1998 edition of the Handbook. Her tireless efforts in making this Handbook a reality are much appreciated. Additional thanks are extended to all those who have endured the countless tasks that were necessary to ensure that the text is well presented including, but most certainly not limited to:

Mark Tamplin, Ph.D., for his review, input and needed revisions;

Prentice Hall and its very capable staff of editors and writers for their countless suggestions, recommendations and input to ensure a very readable and comprehensive text; and

R.R. Donnelley for its timely assistance in organizing the finished product.

Introduction

Eating habits in the United States have changed dramatically in the past twenty years. More than 50% of the food we eat is prepared in restaurants, delicatessens, cafeterias, or institutional kitchens. The danger of eating contaminated food is much greater now due to the increase in the number of people who prepare the food we eat.

The sources for the food we eat have changed, too. Shrimp from the Philippines, grapes from Chile, cheese from France, beef from Uruguay, and kiwi fruit from New Zealand—an international selection of foods that pose new problems for the manager who is purchasing for the food establishment. The hamburger you eat today may have been prepared on the other side of the United States before it was processed, frozen, and shipped to the neighborhood fast-food establishment.

In the United States, the number of **reported cases** of foodborne illness is estimated at 3 million a year. The Food and Drug Administration "estimates 24 to 81 million people become ill from microorganisms in food, resulting in an estimated 10,000 needless deaths every year." Most cases of foodborne illnesses are not reported because people think they have the "flu" or simply do not want to go through the trouble of contacting a physician or the health department. The sad thing about this is that foodborne illness is a preventable disease. By purchasing and serving menu items using safe sanitary practices, it is possible to serve safe food.

The *Handbook for Safe Food Service Management* is designed to provide you with the "need to know" information which can help you become a successful food manager or supervisor. The responsibility for managing a food establishment is enormous. The materials that you are about to study can help you prevent a foodborne illness outbreak.

We hope you find this book useful. The knowledge applied in the area of food service and sanitation is critical to the health and well-being of the people you serve. We salute you in your endeavor and wish you the best in the pursuit of your goals.

CHAPTER 1
Managerial Responsibilities

☞ *As managers/supervisors in food establishments you have responsibilities that extend beyond cost control and profits. The safety of the consumer is and must be your first concern. This safety is determined by the facility itself, the food you serve, and the employees who are under your supervision. It is up to you to ensure that everything possible is done to provide good, safe food.*

Overview

As a manager or supervisor, you must know how to successfully operate a sanitary food establishment. Daily activities include hiring food handlers, purchasing, receiving, planning, storing, maintaining equipment, and overseeing all activities from start to finish. Goals are tied to the "bottom line," and this includes serving safe food. As the person responsible for managing all of these activities, you must understand what has to be done in order to serve safe food.

Role of Manager/Supervisor in Food Establishments

In any establishment that prepares and serves food, the manager is responsible for the sanitation program, direction of personnel, and control of costs. Supervisors and food handlers, who are responsible for helping the manager, need to know how to serve safe food.

In this book, the Hazard Analysis Critical Control Points (HACCP) system is introduced to monitor food from purchase of ingredients to final product. Foodborne illness is a preventable problem. If food is handled correctly, contamination will not occur. Information on HACCP is provided in Chapter 3.

This chapter provides an outline of the specific knowledge, skills, and abilities that a food manager needs to operate a safe food facility. The material in these outlines was developed by the Accreditation Study Committee, Council II, Conference for Food Protection. These are recommendations for the competencies needed by the basic unit manager. The levels and outlines of the two sections in this text are intended to help the basic unit manager identify the scope of work and responsibility of this task.

If you understand that you need to gain this knowledge in order to perform your job, perhaps the material in this book will have more meaning. When you consider the terrible outcomes that are possible when you serve food that is not safe, the importance of learning how to be a responsible manager is enormous.

There are two sections to this outline. Section 1 describes **specific knowledge to be acquired and demonstrated** and is a reference or framework concerning the information you must know to be able to understand how to perform as a manager.

Section 2 describes **specific food safety management knowledge** and refers to the specific knowledge from Section 1 in terms of what the manager should be able to demonstrate in the day-to-day operation of the facility.

Sections 1 and 2 both reflect the standards provided in the current model ordinances, interpretive documents, and Centers for Disease Control statistics concerning factors causing confirmed foodborne illness and foodborne outbreaks. This knowledge must be integrated into the food manager's performance if the incidence of foodborne illness is to be decreased or controlled.

Section 1

Specific Knowledge to Be Acquired and Demonstrated

A certified food manager must be able to acquire and demonstrate competency in the following areas:

I.   **Identify foodborne illness**

Define the terms associated with foodborne illness:
    foodborne illness
    foodborne outbreak
    foodborne infection
    foodborne intoxication
    diseases communicated by food
    foodborne pathogens

Recognize the major microorganisms and toxins that can contaminate food and the problems that can be associated with the contamination:
    bacteria
    viruses
    parasites
    fungi

Define and recognize chemical and physical contamination and associated illnesses.

Define and recognize the major contributing factors for foodborne illness.

Recognize how microorganisms cause foodborne disease.

II. **Identify time/temperature relationship with foodborne illness**

Recognize the relationship between time/temperature and microorganisms (survival, growth, and toxin production) in stages:
    receiving
    storing
    thawing
    cooking
    holding/displaying
    serving
    cooling (post-production)
    reheating
    transporting

Describe the use of thermometers in monitoring food temperatures:
> types of thermometers
> techniques and frequency
> calibration and frequency

III. Describe the relationship between personal hygiene and food safety

Recognize the association between hand contact and foodborne illness:
> handwashing, technique and frequency
> proper use of gloves, including replacement times
> minimizing hand contact with food

Recognize the association of personal habits and behavior to foodborne illness:
> smoking
> eating and drinking
> wearing clothing that may contaminate food
> personal behaviors such as sneezing, coughing, etc.

Recognize how policies, procedures, and management contribute to improved food hygiene practices.

IV. Describe methods for preventing food contamination

Define terms associated with contamination:
> contamination
> adulteration
> damage
> approved source
> sound and safe condition

Identify potential hazards prior to and during delivery:
> approved source
> sound and safe condition

Identify potential hazards and methods to minimize or eliminate hazards after delivery:
> personal hygiene
> cross-contamination
> food to food
> equipment and utensils
> contamination
> chemical
> additives
> physical

Service /display—customer contamination

Storage

Re-service

V. Identify and apply correct procedures for cleaning and sanitizing equipment and utensils

Define terms associated with cleaning and sanitizing:
   cleaning
   sanitizing

Apply appropriate methods of cleaning and sanitizing:
   manual warewashing
   mechanical warewashing
   clean in place

Identify frequency of cleaning and sanitizing.

VI. Recognize problems and potential solutions associated with facility, equipment, and layout

Identify facility, design, and construction suitable for food establishments:
   floors, walls, and ceilings
   pest control
   lighting
   plumbing
   ventilation
   water supply
   wastewater disposal

   Identify equipment and utensil design and location.

VII. Recognize problems and potential solutions associated with housekeeping and maintenance

Implement:
   self-inspection program
   pest control program
   cleaning schedules and procedures
   equipment and facility maintenance program

Section 2

Specific Food Safety Management Knowledge

A certified food manager must be able to demonstrate skills and abilities necessary to perform management functions.

I.   **Assess the potential for foodborne illness in a food establishment**

Perform operational food safety assessment:
>   menu analysis
>   recipe development
>   facility equipment and layout

Recognize standards, policies, and procedures:
>   specifications: written standards, policies, and procedures
>   methods for correct development, monitoring, and verification of policies,
>   including the Hazard Analysis Critical Control Points (HACCP)
>   monitoring program

Select and train employees:
>   principles and practices: site-specific procedures
>   documentation of pertinent employee information

Implement self-audit/inspection program:
>   schedules
>   procedures
>   records

Revise policy and procedure (feedback loop).

Implement crisis management program.

II. **Assess and manage the process flow**

Identify approved source.

Implement and maintain a receiving program:
>   sound and safe condition—inspect the load
>   moving into storage

Implement and maintain storage procedures:
    time/temperature
    protection from contamination
    rotation
    adequate facility and equipment
    monitor

Implement and maintain preparation procedures:
    time/temperature
    personal hygiene
    protection from contamination
    adequate facility and equipment
    monitor

Implement and maintain holding/service/display procedures:
    time/temperature
    personal hygiene
    adequate facility equipment
    protection from contamination
    monitor

Implement and maintain cooling and post-preparation storage procedures:
    time/temperature
    adequate facility and equipment
    protection from contamination
    monitor

Implement and maintain re-service procedures:
    time/temperature
    adequate facility and equipment
    protection from contamination
    monitor

Implement and maintain transportation procedures:
    time/temperature
    adequate facility and equipment
    protection from contamination
    personal hygiene
    monitor

Summary

In Sections 1 and 2, individual managerial tasks and behaviors are identified. The following statements summarize the responsibilities assigned to the food manager.

Routinely responsible for identifying hazards to the public health in the day-to-day operation of a food preparation, service, or dispensing facility.

Routinely develops or implements specific policies, procedures, or standards aimed at preventing foodborne illness.

Responsible for coordinating training, supervising, or directing food preparation activities and taking corrective action as needed to protect the health of the consumer.

Responsible for conducting in-house self-inspections of daily operations on a periodic basis to see that policies and procedures concerning food safety are being followed.

The Accreditation Study Committee defines the manager as "the first-line supervisor." This is the person who deals with the day-to-day responsibilities of food preparation. The competencies (skills and actions) are aimed at the unit manager.

The food industry is a highly demanding field. Management of a food service establishment frequently involves working weekends and late hours. A manager has much to gain from well-trained employees who can assume responsibility. Selecting, training, and evaluating workers is crucial to the operation of a safe food establishment.

A good manager is one who wants and works to make the employees successful. If your employees are successful, you will be, too.

Chapter 1 Review Questions

1.   What is the main responsibility of the food manager and/or supervisor?

2.   According to the Accreditation Study, Conference for Food Protection, the basic food manager is responsible for:

   A.

   B.

   C.

   D.

3.   List the stages in food preparation and service where time and temperature are crucial to keeping food from becoming contaminated:

   A.

   B.

   C.

   D.

   E.

   F.

   G.

   H.

   I.

See Appendix E for answers.

CHAPTER 2
Foodborne Illness

☞ *One of the most important responsibilities of a food manager is to prepare and serve high-quality, safe food. To be successful you need to know what can cause a foodborne illness and how to eliminate it.*

Responsibility of Food Service Managers

Your knowledge of how food becomes contaminated and how to prevent foodborne illness is vital to the success of your job. The FDA Food Code states that every food manager or supervisor is responsible for knowing how foodborne illnesses are caused and prevented.

The FDA Food Code also stresses the importance of recognizing the health conditions of your employees. The Food Code states that the food service manager must require employees to report illnesses that could be transmitted through foods. This also requires the manager to recognize the symptoms of certain transmittable diseases.

According to the U.S. Centers for Disease Control and Prevention (CDC), the following factors contributed to foodborne illnesses traced to food service establishments. You might note that the numbers add up to more than 100%. This is because more than one factor is usually involved in contributing to a foodborne illness outbreak.

63%	Inadequate cooling and cold-holding of food
29%	Preparing food more than 12 hours ahead of serving
27%	Inadequate hot-holding of food
26%	Poor personal hygiene and/or an infected food handler
25%	Inadequate reheating of food
9%	Inadequate cleaning of equipment
7%	Improper use of leftovers
6%	Cross-contamination (hands, cutting boards, utensils, etc.)
5%	Inadequate cooking
4%	Food containers (pots, pans, etc.) that add toxic chemicals to food
2%	Contaminated raw ingredients (such as oysters, meat, and poultry)
2%	Intentionally adding too much chemical food additives
1%	Incidentally adding improper chemical additives
1%	Unsafe sources of food

This is a very important list because these factors are what we use to determine the critical control points in production of food, and they form the basis of a HACCP plan. Refer to this list as you proceed through the book.

Because the goal is to prevent all foodborne illnesses, you must understand **how** and **when** contamination occurs, and you must train your employees to understand why they need to handle food safely to reduce the chance of a foodborne illness.

Sources of Hazards

Food can be contaminated *biologically*, *chemically*, and *physically*. Biological contamination is caused by harmful bacteria, viruses, and parasites. Chemical contamination is caused when substances such as cleaning compounds, food additives, or pesticides get into food. Physical contamination is caused when hair, glass, metal shavings, broken objects, dirt, etc. get into food.

Biological Contamination

Most foodborne illnesses are caused by microorganisms (such as bacteria, viruses, and parasites) that come from people who handle food improperly, and from microorganisms that are already on the food when you receive it.

If food is not handled properly, such as being left in the *danger zone* (41 to 140°F) for too long or not being cooked to the correct temperature, bacteria that cause foodborne illness can quickly multiply to high levels in the food.

Four types of microorganisms cause biological contamination in foods: *bacteria*, *viruses*, *parasites*, and *fungi*. However, the majority of problems are caused by bacteria and viruses. The following information will help you to better understand how to prevent problems that can affect the food you serve to your customer.

Bacteria

Bacteria cause more cases of foodborne illness than any other type of dangerous microorganism. They are found everywhere and can **grow** on food. Other harmful organisms, including viruses and parasites, do not grow on food.

Bacteria grow best when there is plenty of water (moisture), nutrients, a warm temperature (70 to 140°F), and not too much acid present in the food. These types of foods in which harmful bacteria can grow are called **potentially hazardous foods** (PHF's). Examples of PHF's are milk, milk products, eggs, meat, poultry, fish, shellfish, and edible crustacea. Notice that these foods come from animals. However, even cantaloupe and watermelon are classified as hazardous because they have plenty of water, not too much acid, and supply nutrients that bacteria use to grow.

Freezing and drying foods do not kill bacteria. These methods keep bacteria in a dormant or hibernating state. As soon as the food thaws, or water is added to a dehydrated food, the bacteria can continue to grow.

Bacteria can be classified into three groups, depending on whether they need oxygen to grow. This is important because some of the problems that can occur in a food service establishment are affected by the way foods are wrapped or covered. For example, did you know that botulism has been traced to onions that were cooked in oil, then stored too long at room temperature, and to baked potatoes that were wrapped and stored at room temperature?

Anaerobic Bacteria

There are types of bacteria that can live and grow with little or **no oxygen**; these are called *anaerobic* bacteria. Botulism, a severe illness which can lead to death, is caused by anaerobic bacteria called *Clostridium botulinum*. Usually, when foods are cooked, much of the oxygen leaves the food. Examples of places where anaerobic bacteria can grow include canned foods, plastic-wrapped foods, and in the center of large stockpots of food. Also, if you place food in oil, oxygen is kept out and anaerobic bacteria grow quickly. Anaerobic bacteria can also grow in vacuum and modified-atmosphere-packaged foods if they are not properly refrigerated.

Aerobic Bacteria

Some bacteria must have **oxygen** to grow and are called *aerobic* bacteria. They may require a lot of air or just a small amount, but they must have some oxygen to grow. *Pseudomonas* is a type of bacteria that must have oxygen to grow. These bacteria are the ones that usually cause food to spoil. This is why many foods are vacuum or modified-atmosphere packaged to stop aerobic bacteria from spoiling food.

Facultative Bacteria

Unfortunately, most of the bacteria that can cause foodborne illness grow either **with** or **without** air, and are called *facultative bacteria*. Examples of these bacteria are *Salmonella*, *Escherichia coli*, and *Staphylococcus aureus* (staph).

Bacterial Growth

The main reason that bacteria can cause so many foodborne illnesses is that they multiply so fast. Bacteria multiply by cell division. That is, one cell splits into two cells, and those two split into four, and four split to become eight, and so on. In this way bacteria can multiply into millions or billions if hazardous foods are left in the danger zone (41 to 140ºF) for too long.

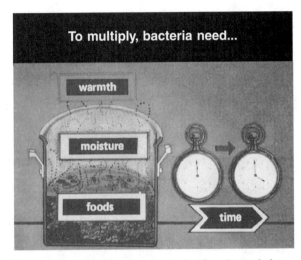

When bacteria are multiplying, they are able to consume the nutrients in foods and they produce waste products. The waste products may be a slime, such as that formed on spoiled meat and fish. However, not all waste products from bacteria are undesirable. The type of bacteria used to form cheeses, yogurts, sour cream, and similar foods are helpful.

Spores

Some bacteria have the ability to change into forms that are very resistant to heat and dry conditions. These are called **spores**. Spores occur when bacteria form a thick "shell." In commercial canning and drying operations, high heat and special procedures are used to destroy spores. Home-canned foods are not produced the same way as commercial foods and are not permitted to be used in food establishments.

Spores are capable of returning to a multiplying form (vegetative state) and causing foodborne illness if they are not destroyed. Later in this book, when vacuum packing is discussed, you will need to remember that inadequate heating can shock a spore into becoming vegetative and growing again.

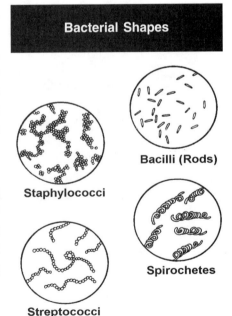

Bacteria also grow in different shapes, as shown in the figure. However, unless you use a microscope, you cannot see individual bacterial cells. Millions of bacteria need to be present before you can see or feel them. For example, the slimy texture of spoiled meat and seafood is caused by the presence of billions of bacteria.

Food Acidity and Alkalinity; pH

Bacteria grow best when the food is **slightly acidic, neutral, or slightly alkaline, and contains enough water for the microorganisms to grow.** The measure of acidity or alkalinity is called the pH. When the pH of a food is less than 7, it is acidic; more than 7, the food is alkaline; at 7 it is neutral.

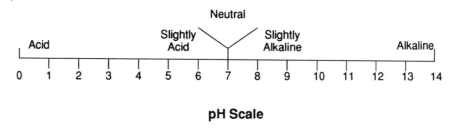

pH Scale

Examples of acidic, neutral, and alkaline foods are listed below.

Acidic	Neutral	Alkaline
Citrus Juices	Milk	Egg White
Mayonnaise	Meat	Soda Crackers
Salad Dressing	Vegetables	Black Olives

The foods near the pH neutral point (pH 7) are ideal for growth of bacteria that cause food infections and food intoxication. For example, meats, poultry, seafood, eggs, and milk do not have very much acid and are labeled as potentially hazardous foods (PHF's). Some vegetables that are also low in acid, such as corn, rice, and peas, are also ideal for bacteria growth once they are cooked.

Foods with a lot of acid do not support bacterial growth. Examples of these highly acidic foods are pickled foods, certain fresh fruits, and citrus.

Water Activity

Just like all living things, bacteria must have enough water to grow and multiply. The amount of water for bacterial growth is called the water activity (A_w). The food must have a water activity level of 0.85 or higher to support bacterial growth. Fresh foods usually have a water activity level between 0.97 to 0.99, which allows growth of harmful bacteria. Freezing, drying, or adding salt or sugar reduces the amount of available water and slows or prevents bacterial growth. This is why salt or sugar are added to some foods to preserve them; the salt and sugar hold the water tightly and do not allow bacteria to use it to grow and spoil the food.

Bacterial Growth Rate

When bacteria have the right conditions for growth, they multiply in a very distinct pattern. During the early stage, known as the **lag phase**, growth is very slow. You can keep potentially hazardous foods in the **lag phase** by properly refrigerating food and keeping it out of the danger zone (41 to 140°F).

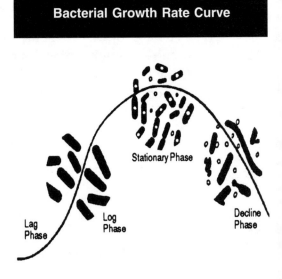

Bacterial Growth Rate Curve

Stationary Phase

Lag Phase

Log Phase

Decline Phase

The next stage of bacterial growth is known as the **log or exponential phase.** This is where bacterial growth is **very** rapid. Next, when bacteria have used up the nutrients, they reach the **stationary phase** and multiplication slows down. Finally, they reach the **decline phase** and bacteria begin to die.

As discussed above, a food must have nutrients, not too much acid, and enough water for bacteria to grow. Therefore, there is very little we can do to control these factors. We can, however, **control time and temperature to limit bacterial growth!** Of course, you cannot eliminate all bacteria from the environment; they are everywhere. But you **can** limit the growth of harmful bacteria to relatively safe levels.

Viruses

There are two important concepts to know about foodborne viruses that affect people. First, they do not multiply in foods, only in the cells of humans. Second, almost all foodborne illnesses are traced to workers who are infected with the virus and do not wash their hands after using the rest room. Consequently, epidemiological reports show that foods that are not cooked after handling, such as salads, are associated with viral foodborne illness.

A food handler can excrete viruses in feces, urine, or through a respiratory tract infection. Failure to wash hands after going to the rest room, coughing, sneezing, and wiping a runny nose are ways to spread contamination. A worker **must always wash** his or her hands after these actions.

A variety of viruses can be spread through food contaminated by the food handler. One serious illness is **hepatitis A** (also known as **infectious hepatitis**). Symptoms of hepatitis A include fever, vomiting, jaundice, nausea, and cramps. The symptoms can last from several weeks to several months. An employee diagnosed with hepatitis A should not return to work until approval is obtained from the proper local health department. Cases of hepatitis A must be reported to the supervisor.

Raw shellfish from polluted waters are also a frequent source of viral illnesses. They are usually contaminated because shellfish are harvested from sewage-polluted waters. Both hepatitis A virus and Norwalk virus have caused numerous illnesses to people who ate contaminated raw shellfish, such as clams and oysters.

Norwalk virus is believed to cause a very large amount of all viral illness. It lives in the human intestinal tract and contaminates feces. Most Norwalk viral illness occurs in the fall and winter months, much like the flu and common cold. Consequently, this is the time of the year when food service workers might accidentally contaminate foods and when raw shellfish might contain the virus.

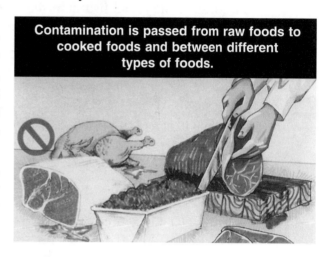

Contamination is passed from raw foods to cooked foods and between different types of foods.

Raw vegetables, prepared salads, raw shellfish, and contaminated water may be the source of foodborne illness caused by Norwalk virus. Symptoms of Norwalk illness are nausea, vomiting, diarrhea, abdominal pain, headache, and low-grade fever, occurring 24 to 48 hours after consumption of food or water contaminated by the virus. High standards of hygiene or thorough cooking can eliminate this hazard.

The most likely foods to transmit viral illness are those that receive no heating after handling. Salads, sandwiches, milk, water, sliced luncheon meats, fruits, bakery products, raw or uncooked oysters and clams, and desserts are such foods.

Parasites

Parasites are organisms that live within or feed off another organism. They are many times larger than bacteria and viruses. Foods such as pork, fish, and beef can contain parasites. If food is not cooked to a temperature high enough to kill the parasite, or frozen for a specified number of days, humans can become infected.

In humans, the disease caused by infected pork is called **trichinosis**. Fortunately, most of us know that pork should be cooked until well done. If not, the trichina worm can survive, enter the body, and become lodged in muscle tissue. This can lead to chronic pain.

Certain types of infected fish can cause a disease termed **anisakiasis**. The parasite grows in warm-blooded marine mammals such as walruses, seals, and sea lions, and infects fish that spend all, or part, of their lives in fresh water. If these types of fish are eaten raw, the parasite can cause an illness sometimes termed "sushi stomach." It is rarely fatal but can cause great discomfort. Parasites such as the *Anisakis* worm will be killed if the fish is cooked, frozen at -4°F or below for 7 days in a freezer, or -31°F for 15 hours in a blast freezer.

The danger from all parasites in food can be eliminated through proper cooking. Cook all meat, poultry, and fish until the internal temperature reaches the approved or safe temperature for the required time to avoid parasitic foodborne disease. Be sure to check internal temperatures in several different parts of the meat.

Fungi

Fungi include *molds*, *yeasts*, and *mushrooms*. Certain types of fungi can be poisonous to humans.

Molds

Mold is a natural part of many food products, such as cheeses. Molds rarely cause foodborne illness but are responsible for much food spoilage. They are very adaptable organisms and grow well on all types of foods. They grow in moist or dry conditions, at low and high temperatures, and at a wide range of pH. The fuzzy, often highly colored growth of molds is easily blown through the air to other foods. Foods are spoiled by molds, which produce "musty" odors and destroy the fresh flavor of foods.

Certain molds produce toxins which have been associated with foodborne illness, although this is very rare. Foods that can be contaminated by fungal toxins include grains, breads, and nuts. For example, in certain grain products, such as peanuts, a mold termed *Aspergillus* can produce a toxin called **aflatoxin**. If present in a very high dose, this toxin produces toxic effects in humans. However, there is very low risk of human illness because industry and public health agencies do an excellent job of closely monitoring aflatoxin in foods.

Freezing prevents growth of molds but has no effect on the mold spores that are already present in the food. Heating to 140°F for 10 minutes will destroy molds but not any toxins that might be present. Proper temperatures in cooking, cooling, and storage prevent the growth of fungi.

Yeasts

Yeasts are used in the production of bread and the processing of beer and wine. They are not known to cause illness when present in foods. However, yeasts can cause foods such as sauerkraut, fruit juices, syrups, molasses, honey, jellies, meats, beer, and wine to spoil. Yeasts are easily killed by heating food products to 136°F for 15 minutes and can be controlled with proper cleaning and sanitizing.

Store high–acid (tart or sour) foods in approved containers.

Chemical Contamination

If not properly handled, food products, equipment, and preparation areas can all be contaminated by chemical substances. Most reported chemical contamination is associated with substances such as food additives and preservatives, pesticides, toxic metals, and toxic cleaning products.

Symptoms of chemical food poisoning can occur within seconds of ingesting the chemical. Initial symptoms include vomiting and diarrhea.

Food Additives

Additives and preservatives are agents that enhance the flavor of food products or keep them fresh longer. However, some additives, such as sulfites, can make some people extremely ill, especially those with asthma.

Government and industry standards prohibit the use of sulfites by food service establishments. Sulfites are still used in food processing but are tightly regulated. Check with your local public health department for state or local regulations regarding sulfites.

Food processors must label products clearly when any type of additive is present. Some states require notices on menus or signs if sulfites are in the menu item. By limiting the use of products with additives in your establishment, you can reduce the danger to your customers. If you do use additives, be sure to clearly LABEL products so that there is no confusion!

Pesticides

Pesticides used on crops to control insect damage, or insecticides used in your food service operation to kill roaches and other unwanted insects, can be harmful if used in excessively high amounts. Poisoning due to pesticides is usually a result of carelessness, mislabeling, and poor housekeeping procedures.

Toxic Metals

Toxic metals such as copper, brass, cadmium, lead, and zinc can be a source of chemical contamination.

If acidic foods are stored in galvanized food containers, **zinc** can leach into the food and make it poisonous. Fruit juices, pickles, and other acidic foods must never be placed in galvanized containers!

Some refrigerator shelves contain **cadmium,** which could contaminate food. Therefore, you should never put unprotected food directly on refrigerator shelves where cadmium could leach into the food.

Toxic Housekeeping Products

Improper storage and use of cleaning agents, sanitizers, and other substances can also result in chemical contamination of food. Keep only chemicals that are needed for cleaning, sanitizing, and pest control. Be sure to store them in clearly designated places and be sure they are placed in a **PROPERLY LABELED** container. Too many problems have occurred when someone mistook household cleaner for sugar!

Physical Contamination

Physical contamination occurs when objects such as glass, hair, nails, jewelry, metal fragments, or even dirt become mixed with food. The use of broken or worn utensils and equipment can be a source of physical contamination in foods.

Improper ventilation and poorly maintained facilities can contribute to direct physical contamination. If you do not regularly clean your kitchen vents, they can blow objects into the food (for example, large amounts of fungal spores, hair, dirt, etc.).

Improperly maintained plumbing pipes, such as those in walk-in cold rooms, can also drip contaminated substances (for example, water, fungi, metal, paint, dirt, etc.)

Cross-contamination

Contaminated or uncooked raw foods can cause harmful microorganisms to be passed to safe foods and cause a foodborne illness. This is called *cross-contamination*. For example, cross-contamination occurs when juices from raw food items, such as meats, poultry, and seafoods, touch or drip onto cooked foods. Cross-contamination also occurs when food contact surfaces (such as cutting boards) are not kept clean and sanitized.

Also, although they are not necessarily hazardous foods, vegetables and fruits can also carry bacteria that come from the soil and cross-contaminate foods with disease-causing microorganisms. For example, if you use a cutting board to cut up fruit or vegetables, you must clean and sanitize the board and knife before they touch other cooked foods. If not, you could be cross-contaminating the food preparation surface with a microorganism called *Clostridium perfringens*

Another example of possible cross-contamination occurs when raw chicken is trimmed on a cutting board, fried in a pan, then returned to the unsanitized cutting board to be cubed. In this way you have contaminated your cooked (safe) chicken with bacteria from the raw chicken.

Remember that *all* raw products can carry harmful bacteria, and that **cross-contamination is one of the major causes of foodborne illness.**

Common Causes of Foodborne Illnesses

When people speak of foodborne illness, it can be either a **food infection** or a **food intoxication**. A **foodborne infection** is caused by eating live harmful microorganisms that multiply in the body and cause disease. You normally do not know you are sick for 1 to 2 days while the bacteria are multiplying in your body.

Another type of foodborne illness is **foodborne intoxication**. In this case, bacteria have already produced a toxin in the food before it is eaten. This is why staph food poisoning happens so fast. Symptoms usually occur within 1 to 6 hours, and include nausea, vomiting, diarrhea, and intestinal cramps. Botulism is a foodborne intoxication and is one of the deadliest foodborne diseases known.

In the following section, we describe the most common microorganisms that cause foodborne illness.

Bacterial Food Infection

Salmonella

Each year *Salmonella* bacteria are estimated to cause over 2 million foodborne infections. They are found in the intestines of many people as well as in other animals, such as rodents, dogs, cats, ducks, and chickens. They also live in the intestines of salamanders, alligators, turtles, and many other cold-blooded animals. Cockroaches and flies can also carry *Salmonella* around the kitchen.

Some people can even carry the *Salmonella* organism and not know it. This is dangerous because they don't know that they can make other people sick if they do not wash their hands.

Salmonella can also be found in poultry, red meats, shellfish, and eggs. They usually get on these raw foods in the slaughterhouse. Eggs, however, are different. *Salmonella* can even be inside the egg when it is laid.

Under the right conditions (on potentially hazardous foods) *Salmonella* bacteria can grow rapidly and cause *salmonellosis*, a serious foodborne illness. Dishes that are prepared from these foods, such as chicken salad, egg salad, ham salad, or egg custards, have been known to cause salmonellosis.

Salmonella can also contaminate foods during processing either before or after they are purchased. Cross-contamination from poor personal hygiene on the part of food workers, and failure to work with clean, sanitized cutting boards, equipment, cloths, and utensils, can also cause *Salmonella* infection.

Most cases of salmonellosis begin within 12 to 36 hours after contaminated food has been eaten. Nausea, vomiting, cramps, and fever are symptoms of the illness. Salmonellosis can cause death in a person with a weak immune system or in an elderly person.

Shigella

Another microorganism, *Shigella*, is also found in the intestines of humans. Most foodborne illnesses caused by this organism result from not washing your hands after using the rest room and then touching a food that will not be cooked. This can cause *shigellosis*. It can be killed easily by cooking; however, it is usually transmitted by prepared foods, such as potato, tuna, turkey, and macaroni salads, gravies, and milk products.

Symptoms usually begin from 6 to 72 hours after the food is eaten and include diarrhea, fever, chills, and dehydration.

Escherichia coli

Escherichia coli is found in the intestines of all humans and warm-blooded animals. This is why public health agencies use the presence of *Escherichia coli* to determine when human or animal waste has contaminated food or water. Although most types of *Escherichia coli* do not cause illness, some can cause serious diseases. You have probably learned about a new type of *Escherichia coli* termed *O157:H7* that can be found in ground beef products and cause a very serious illness in children and the elderly if hamburger is not cooked to an internal temperature of 155°F. Also, the disease termed "traveler's diarrhea," or "Montezuma's revenge," is caused by a type of *Escherichia coli* that produces a potent diarrhea-causing toxin.

Symptoms of *Escherichia coli* illness are severe diarrhea, cramping, and dehydration. The illness can occur within 12 to 24 hours after contaminated food is eaten. Thorough cooking and reheating, good sanitation, and refrigeration at 41°F or below are important control measures.

Yersinia

Yersinia is a bacterium that causes **yersiniosis**. It is found in the intestines of animals and humans. After a food is contaminated by *Yersinia*, the bacteria continue to multiply even at temperatures below 41°F. However, thorough heating will destroy it. THIS IS WHY REHEATING FOODS TO 165°F IS VERY IMPORTANT.

You can prevent *Yersinia* contamination through proper handwashing, safe food handling practices, and cooking at the required temperature.

The symptoms of yersiniosis appear 3 to 7 days after the contaminated food is eaten and include fever, headache, nausea, abdominal pain, and diarrhea.

Listeria

Listeria bacteria can cause **listeriosis** in animals and humans. They are found EVERY-WHERE. *Listeria* is naturally found in soil, water, animal feed, and in the intestines of humans and animals. They are also found in meat, unpasteurized or improperly pasteurized milk and milk products (such as soft unpasteurized cheeses), and vegetables grown in contaminated soil.

A unique feature of *Listeria* bacteria is that they can grow even in a refrigerator set at 41°F. A recent scientific study found that 70% of refrigerators in the United States have *Listeria*. They especially like to live in cooked deli meats, such as hot dogs and sandwich meats. Also, *Listeria* can be found in moist places in walk-in cold rooms and refrigerators. The best way to prevent *Listeria* is to keep all storage areas DRY and CLEAN.

Listeriosis can sometimes be a deadly disease. Symptoms might include sudden onset of fever, chills, headache, backache, abdominal pain, and diarrhea. Listeriosis is especially deadly for people with suppressed immune systems and the elderly. It is estimated that each year, almost 1000 miscarriages, stillbirths, or birth defects are caused by *Listeria* ingested by pregnant women.

Campylobacter fetus jejuni

Campylobacter fetus jejuni is believed to be one of the leading causes of foodborne infection. This organism is frequently found in beef, pork, lamb, poultry, unpasteurized milk, and sometimes in contaminated raw vegetables.

Symptoms usually occur within 2 to 10 days and include abdominal pain, nausea, fever, and headache. Bloody diarrhea is common and the symptoms may last from 2 to 7 days.

Vibrio parahaemolyticus

Vibrio parahaemolyticus is a common bacterium which thrives in seawater. It is a natural part of seawater and is caused by pollution. However, this microorganism is one of the most common causes of bacterial foodborne infections caused by seafoods. Seafoods that carry *V. parahaemolyticus* include oysters, shrimp, and blue crabs.

The disease is typically transmitted by cross-contamination where cooked products are contaminated with seawater, raw seafood, or contaminated hands. This bacterium is very unique because it can multiply every 9 minutes, compared to 20 minutes for most other bacteria. Therefore, if cross-contamination occurs, it can multiply to very high and dangerous levels in a very short period of time.

Symptoms usually include abdominal pain, diarrhea, nausea, and vomiting within 12 hours after eating the contaminated food. The disease lasts 2 to 5 days.

Bacterial Food Intoxication

Food intoxication occurs when a toxin is already present in the food at the time it is eaten. These illnesses are caused by certain bacteria with this special ability.

Staphylococcus aureus

Staphylococcal food intoxication is a common foodborne illness. It is caused by toxin produced by the *Staphylococcus* microorganism. This bacterium is found on the skin, nose, and mouth of 50 to 70% of all people. It is easily transmitted by sneezing, coughing, scratching skin, and touching hair. Once on food, *Staphylococcus* can grow and produce a toxin.

Wounds, cuts, burns, and infections in the nose or sinuses, and pimples, are common places where staphylococcal microorganisms thrive. Food managers should watch for these problems in their employees. Employees with severe cuts, wounds, or burns must make certain their injuries are properly bandaged and that an effective barrier, such as a disposable glove, is worn when handling food. Employees with infected cuts, burns, or boils should be excluded from all food handling (not even with gloves) and warewashing (dishes, utensils, pans, etc.).

Staph is also unique because it can grow on foods that do not have a lot of water, such as foods with high amounts of sugar (custards, desserts) and salt (hams). This is why foods commonly involved in staphylococcal food intoxication include ham products, cold meats, salads, custards, meat and meat products, milk products, and cream-filled desserts. The organism can also be transferred to food by improperly sanitized food preparation equipment.

Foods contaminated with staphylococcal microorganisms are usually those which require a lot of handling during preparation. Potentially hazardous foods (PHFs) that are left too long in the danger zone (41 to 140°F) are at risk because **once staph produces the toxin, it cannot be destroyed by cooking or reheating!**

However, the growth of this bacterium and its toxin can be reduced by:

- Keeping potentially hazardous foods below 41°F or above 140°F

- Not allowing foods to remain at room temperature

- Moving foods through the danger zone quickly

- Cooling foods in shallow pans

Symptoms of this intoxication appear quickly, usually within 2 to 4 hours, and include nausea, severe vomiting, diarrhea, cramps, chills, sweating, headache, and severe fatigue. The effects of staphylococcal food poisoning last for 1 or 2 days.

Bacillus cereus

Bacillus cereus is very common in soils where vegetables and grains are grown. It is one of a group of bacteria that can form spores. These spores allow the bacteria to survive when there is not enough water and food. This can cause special problems for the food industry because typical cooking temperatures do not kill spore-forming bacteria. This is why PROPER COOLING and HOT-HOLDING are very critical for the control of this and many other foodborne bacteria!

Nearly all cases of *B. cereus* food poisoning are traced to cooked rice that has been improperly cooled or hot-held. Other foods, such as potatoes, pasta, green beans, vegetable sprouts, and dry spices, may contain this microorganism. Many cases have been caused by cooking rice, then leaving it in the cooker at room temperature for more than 4 hours. Under these conditions, *B. cereus* can produce a toxin that enters the rice and causes a foodborne illness. Proper refrigeration and hot-holding solves this problem. Also, keeping dry food products away from moisture will help.

Symptoms of the illness begin from 1 to 16 hours after the contaminated product is eaten and include nausea, vomiting, and diarrhea.

Clostridium botulinum

Clostridium botulinum is the microorganism which causes **botulism**. This bacterium forms spores and grows only where there is no air (anaerobic). The microorganism is found in the soil, in lake and ocean bottoms, and in the intestines of humans, fish, and animals. The bacteria produces a toxin which causes food intoxication.

Foods that can be contaminated by this bacterium include canned or vacuum-packed foods (meats, fish, and vegetables) that do not contain very much acid (low-acid foods), smoked meats (fish, ham, and sausage), and condiments such as chili peppers, tomato relish, and chili. Freezing will not destroy the botulinum spores.

Over the years, botulism has commonly occurred with home-canned or preserved foods that are not processed correctly or when the cans have become severely damaged after processing. Severely dented cans, cans with bulging tops, or "flipper cans" (ones in which the end of the can springs back when pushed on) might all contain botulism toxin. The contaminated food can appear normal or can look slimy and cheesy with a bad smell. So do not rely on smell or sight to decide if the food is safe.

Today, we know of new ways that botulism has caused problems for food service establishments. For example, botulism poisoning has been caused when onions were grilled in oil, stored at room temperature, and then served to customers. Another case involved potatoes that were baked, wrapped, and then stored at room temperature. Proper refrigeration and hot holding would have solved all of these problems.

Symptoms of botulism food poisoning appear within 12 to 36 hours after the contaminated food is eaten and include nausea, diarrhea, vomiting, abdominal pain, headache, dizziness, fatigue, double vision, and difficulty in breathing. Death due to respiratory failure may occur unless quick medical attention is given with prompt administration of the antitoxin medicine.

Clostridium perfringens

Clostridium perfringens is a **very** common bacterium that is found in soil, dust, air, sewage, and the intestines of humans and animals. *C. perfringens* illness can be both a food intoxication and an infection. Contaminated meat and poultry products, especially stews, gravies, sauces, meat pies, and casseroles, are the main source of food poisoning from this spore-forming bacteria.

C. perfringens contamination is a result of improper cooking, cooling, and reheating of foods. It can also be caused by poorly cleaned fresh vegetables. Reheating does not destroy all of the bacteria. Therefore, meat dishes should always be kept out of the temperature danger zone (41 to 140°F).

In healthy individuals, *C. perfringens* causes a fairly mild illness with symptoms of nausea, cramps, and diarrhea. *C. perfringens* food poisoning causes between 10 and 15% of all foodborne illness in the United States. Symptoms occur 8 to 22 hours after the contaminated food has been eaten.

Seafood Toxins

Some fish and shellfish can become poisonous. For example, mussels and clams can become toxic when they eat or filter poisonous types of plankton (microscopic plants and animals) found in water. However, this and most other marine toxins are not destroyed by cooking. This is why you should never eat shellfish during a "red tide."

We depend on government agencies to check shellfish-harvesting waters to detect when red tides are present. This is why it is important for you to purchase seafoods from approved suppliers.

Scombroid Poisoning

Scombroid poisoning is a common cause of seafood illness. Scombroid poisoning occurs when fish such as mahi mahi (dolphinfish), tuna, mackerel, bluefish, and amberjack are not properly refrigerated and begin to spoil. However, not much spoilage is needed to produce scombroid toxin in fish meat. This is another reason why your best protection is to buy seafoods from a reputable dealer.

The spoilage process that produces scombroid toxin happens in fish that have high amounts of the amino **histidine** in their tissues. If these fish are not refrigerated quickly when they are caught, histidine is changed to **histamine**. This is the same toxin that causes symptoms in an allergy attack.

Symptoms occur within minutes to 2 hours of eating the fish and last from 4–6 hours to 1–2 days. The first symptoms are very similar to an allergy attack. Symptoms include redness of the face, sweating, burning feelings in the tongue and mouth, dizziness, nausea, and headache. Later symptoms are rashes, hives, and diarrhea.

Unfortunately, you cannot smell any difference in fish that have scombroid toxin, and the toxin **cannot be destroyed** by freezing, cooking, smoking, curing, or canning.

Ciguatera Poisoning

Ciguatera is also one of the most common causes of seafood poisoning. The toxin is not produced by the fish but from what the fish eats. This is another toxin that is not destroyed by cooking, freezing, or canning.

Certain tropical reefs in the Pacific Ocean and throughout the Caribbean have a type of algae (microscopic plant) that lives on the reef and contains **ciguatoxin**. Small fish eat the algae, then larger fish eat them, and so on, until the largest fish on the reef contain the most toxin. Most local commercial fishermen know the reefs to avoid. However, ciguatoxin poisoning is often caused by fish (such as barracuda and amberjack) bought from a recreational fisherman who did not know that he or she was fishing on a toxic reef.

Symptoms usually occur 4 to 8 hours after eating the fish and include weakness and nervous system disorders. Symptoms can last a long time because the toxin persists in body fat. Remember to buy your fish from a reputable dealer!

Plant Toxins

Plants which are poisonous include water hemlock, fava beans, rhubarb leaves, and jimpson weed. Mushrooms used in food establishments must be from an approved source because of the difficulty in judging between safe and unsafe varieties.

FOODBORNE DISEASE TABLE

DISEASE OR ORAGANISM	INCUBATION	SOURCE	FOODS INVOLVED	CONTROL MEASURES
Salmonellosis (*Salmonella*)	5–72 hours	Feces of infected domestic or wild animals	Meat, poultry, eggs, and their products	Chill foods rapidly, cook food thoroughly, use pasteurized egg products and milk, avoid cross-contamination from raw to cooked foods, wash hands, sanitize equipment
Vibrio Vulnificus	16 hours	Oysters, seawater sediment, plankton	Raw or lightly cooked seafood (i.e., oysters)	Properly cook all seafood, avoid cross-contamination
Escherichia coli (*E. coli* 0157:H7)	3–4 days	Internal tract of cattle, contaminated water	Raw and undercooked ground beef and red meats	Cook to proper internal temperature; with sewage, avoid raw and cooked cross-contamination; practice good personal hygiene; properly clean and sanitize equipment, utensils, and surfaces
Staphylococcal (staph)	1–7 hours	Man is the primary source of contaminates, cooked foods, meats	Cream-filled pastries, custards, sandwich fillings, dressings	Chill foods rapidly, practice good personal hygiene, sanitize equipment, avoid direct hand contact
Botulism	12–36 hours	Soil, mud, water, and intestinal tract of animals	Improperly canned foods, smoked fish vacuum-packed foods	Properly canned foods, cook foods thoroughly, refrigerate at proper temperatures
Clostridium Perfringens	8–24 hours	Feces of infected person and animals, soil, dust, and sewage	Cooked meat and poultry left at room temperature too long, gravy, stew, meat pies	Chill foods rapidly, good personal hygiene, hold-hot foods at 140°F or above, cure meat properly, dispose of sewage properly
Shigellosis (*shigella*)	1–7 days	Feces of infected person, contaminated water	Moist, mixed foods	Practice good personal hygiene, chill foods rapidly, cook food thoroughly, protect and treat water, control flies
Scomboid poisoning	Few minutes to an hour	Fish meat	Scombroid fish (tuna, mackerel, skipjack)	Refrigerate, eat soon after being caught
Ciguatera poisoning	3–24 hours	Several species of seafood caught near shores and reefs	Fish, oysters, clams	Avoid eating liver, intestines, roe, and gonads of tropical fish
Infectious hepatitis A	10–50 days	Feces, urine, blood, of infected person, contaminated water	Shellfish, ready-to-eat, foods handled improperly	Cook food thoroughly, purchase from approved sources, dispose of sewage properly, practice good personal hygiene, avoid hand contact with foods
Trichinosis	4–28 hours	Meat of infected animals	Pork, bear, dog	Cook food thoroughly, cure meats adequately, freeze properly

Source: Bryan, Frank L. *Diseases Transmitted by Foods,* U.S. Department of Health, Education, and Welfare, Public Health Service, Centers for Disease Control Bureau of Training.

Preventing Foodborne Illnesses in Your Establishment

Most foodborne illness occurs because of time/temperature abuse, cross-contamination, and/ or poor personal hygiene. Every food service worker must become health conscious. Training employees in basic hygiene is vital to the safety of the food served in your establishment.

Employee Health

Everyone who handles food should be healthy. Food service employees should never be on duty when they have symptoms of diseases that can be transmitted when they directly contact food or other persons.

The FDA Food Code recommends that managers recognize the signs and symptoms of certain employee illnesses that could be transmitted by foods. This is because some of these diseases are important enough to exclude the person from handling foods.

The manager should know if an employee:

- Has an illness diagnosed as *S. typhi, Shigella* spp., *E. coli* O157:H7, or hepatitis

- Has specific symptoms of illnesses and therefore should not work with exposed food, clean equipment, utensils, and linens

- Had past infections caused by *S. typhi, Shigella* spp., *E. coli* O157:H7, and hepatitis

- Has a high risk of becoming ill from previous exposure to contaminated foods or an infected person.

If so, these employees should be excluded from the food service establishment until they are no longer infectious.

Employees who show signs of illness such as fever, sneezing, coughing, vomiting, diarrhea, or oozing burns and cuts, should be reassigned or sent home and not return to work until they are no longer sick and do not risk passing along their disease.

People can also be **carriers** of disease-producing microorganisms and not be

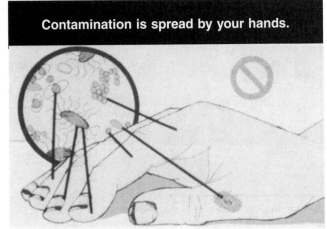

Contamination is spread by your hands.

sick themselves. They may never show the symptoms or they may have recovered, but they can pass on the microorganisms that could make your customers ill. Contact your public health department if you want further information about possible carriers of disease micro-organisms.

Food contamination can occur when a food service employee gets cut while working with food. Blood contaminates food and any surface it touches. Food exposed to blood must be thrown out and surfaces must be sanitized before being used again.

Employees in food establishments are at high risk for cuts, burns, and abrasions. For this reason, first-aid supplies are needed.

Workers who have small cuts, abrasions, or burns and continue to work must cover the wound with a water-resistant bandage. However, bandages on fingers are difficult to keep clean and can hold microorganisms from raw foods that will cross-contaminate cooked foods. Therefore, bandages should be changed often and covered with water-resistant material, or plastic gloves worn.

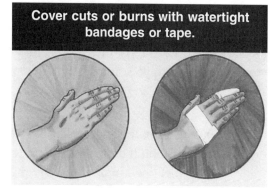

Cover cuts or burns with watertight bandages or tape.

However, more serious cuts and burns are likely to be infected and can be a more serious problem when the employee handles food. An infection may be present and fluids can con-taminate foods and equipment. Food handlers who suffer a severe burn or cut, or workers with infected wounds, cuts, boils, or burns, should not be working with food until their injury has healed. Meanwhile, they may be able to work at other job stations.

No employee who has a disease that can be transmitted by foods, such as an infected boil, infected wound, or an acute respiratory infection, can work in food service areas.

Researchers have concluded that the HIV microorganism that causes AIDS is not spread by food. According to the U.S. Centers for Disease Control, food service workers infected with AIDS should not be restricted from work unless they have another infection or illness.

Personal Hygiene

Practicing good health habits (personal hygiene) is the first step in staying healthy and keeping food safe. All food service workers should take a bath daily with soap and water, and arrive at work clean. Workers should cover their mouths and noses when coughing or sneezing and then *wash their hands* before handling food. This helps reduce the spread of disease (such as staphylococcal food poisoning) by droplet contamination. Employers should also eliminate unsanitary habits, such as scratching the head or touching the mouth or nose, which may pass bacteria on to food.

A person who has a skin infection is a threat to your establishment unless they practice good personal hygiene. They are usually not sick enough to stay away from work and the infection is spread by bacteria that stays on their skin or in their nose and throat. The food and equipment they come into contact with can become contaminated. They must wash their hands thoroughly and frequently.

Activities such as eating, drinking, and tobacco use in any form should be prohibited around exposed foods, clean equipment, utensils, and linens. The Food Code allows employees to drink from a **closed** beverage container, as long as they prevent contamination of the container, hands, or exposed foods, clean equipment, utensils, and linens. It is important to check with your local health department to make sure that this is acceptable in your jurisdiction.

Eating, drinking, and tobacco use are prohibited in food preparation areas to prevent the hand-to-mouth contact which leads to contamination of food. Chewing gum is also a source of droplet contamination. Blowing bubbles or touching the gum with their fingers is prohibited. Employees should eat, drink, and smoke only in designated areas. No employee should resume work after eating, drinking, or smoking without first thoroughly washing his or her hands.

Another common source of contamination is sweat. Food handlers should be careful not to drip sweat onto equipment or into food products. Change gloves at regular intervals to avoid sweat dripping down the arms and onto food. Do not wipe sweat with your hand and then touch food. Do not use wiping cloths which are used on food contact surfaces to wipe your sweat. Use a disposable towel or napkin to wipe away sweat, and then wash your hands.

Do not wipe your hands on work aprons, and then touch food. Freshly washed aprons should always be worn. Dirty aprons contain dangerous bacteria.

Hair should be properly restrained to prevent contamination of food. Remember, staphylococcal food poisoning organisms live on hair. Local regulations will determine exactly what type of hair restraint should be used.

Hand Washing

Most microorganisms that cause foodborne illness are transmitted to foods by the hands of food service workers. Contamination, such as soil from unclean surfaces, chemicals from cleaning products, or viruses and bacteria, can be picked up by the hands.

Hands and arms should always be kept clean. Remember that human skin is never free of bacteria. Skin has all the right ingredients for bacterial growth: moisture, protein, medium pH, and warm temperature. The same is true for the mouth, nose, eyes, throat, and ears. For this reason, the basic practice of **hand washing is perhaps the most important action that you can take to prevent the spread of disease!**

One-half of all healthy people carry staphylococcus on their skin, nose or mouth without showing any signs of an illness. Higher levels of staph can be found in pimples, acne, a skin wound, or inflamed skin.

A food service establishment must provide places for workers to wash their hands frequently. A number of hand sinks should be conveniently located near rest rooms, next to food preparation areas, and wherever needed and kept accessible at all times. These sinks, which are to be used **only** for hand washing, must have warm water, a supply of hand-cleansing soap, and a sanitary means of hand drying, such as disposable towels or an air-drying device. **Do not dry hands on a towel used by anyone else. Do not wash your hands in a food preparation sink.**

Gloves can cause contamination just like hands can. Even if you wear gloves, you and all workers must wash your hands thoroughly before putting on gloves and handling or serving food.

You must also wash your hands and change gloves after any action that might cause contamination: after using the toilet, smoking or eating, coughing or sneezing, touching the hair or face, handling raw poultry or meat, picking objects up from the floor, answering the telephone, or handling soiled dishes.

In addition to hand washing, be careful about touching soiled or infected objects, including clothing. Do not wipe hands on aprons. Aprons are a means of clothing protection **only**. When you wipe your hands on the apron and leave food particles, bacteria begin to multiply on the cloth. The next time you wipe your hands on the apron, they become contaminated.

Hands and fingers should be kept away from face, nose, mouth, and hair. Fingernails should be short, well-trimmed, and clean. Microorganisms caught under long nails can get into food that is being prepared.

Be sure to rub hands and exposed arms with an approved cleaning compound for at least 20 seconds, then rinse with clean water. Pay special attention to areas under fingernails and between fingers, where contamination is most difficult to remove.

Steps for Hand Washing

- Use warm running water.

- Wet hands and arms up to the elbows.

- Apply soap or detergent.

- Rub hands and forearms briskly for at least 20 seconds to build up a good lather. Scrub between fingers and clean nails. If a hand or nail brush is used, make sure the brush is clean and replaced often.

- Rinse thoroughly under running water.
  (The FDA Food Code recommends that hands be washed a second time before drying.)

- Dry hands and arms using a single service towel or hot-air dryer.

After you wash your hands following using the rest room, they may become contaminated again when you touch the door on the way back to the kitchen. You must wash your hands again before preparing food.

Note: Rings, bracelets, and other jewelry trap microorganisms and are very difficult to keep clean. The best way to prevent contamination from jewelry-borne microorganisms is not to wear jewelry when handling food.

Clothing

Dirty clothing presents two problems: odor and contamination by bacteria. Every effort must be made to reduce the risk of passing contamination from clothing to others by food handlers.

Dirt can enter the establishment on employee's shoes or clothing. Ordinary dirt contains many microorganisms from sewage, fertilizer, pesticides, or street soil.

Teach your employees the importance of clean clothing on the job. Employees should arrive at work in clean clothes. They should wear a clean uniform or protective clothing whenever necessary. Caps, nets, or other hair restraints which minimize touching hair should be worn to prevent contamination from loose hair.

If employees wear uniforms or protective clothing provided by the establishment, there should be a locker room or other suitable changing area. It must be separate from the food preparation areas. All employee belongings, including medicines, lunches, coats and purses, must be stored in a designated area away from food, kitchenware, and stored goods.

Summary

There are a number of ways in which food can become contaminated. Some foods are more hazardous than others, and certain ways you handle foods can lead to the spread of contamination. The important thing to remember is that foodborne illness can be prevented through proper procedures in storing, preparing, and serving food. The most crucial elements are **time, temperature, cross-contamination, personal hygiene and habits, along with cleaning and sanitizing**.

Chapter 2 Review Questions

1. Define foodborne illness:

2. Major sources of food contamination are _____ , _____ , and _____ .

3. How does cross-contamination occur?

4. Define the phrase "potentially hazardous food."

5. What conditions do bacteria need in order to grow?

    A.

    B.

    C.

    D.

6. The "lag phase" of bacterial growth refers to:

    A.   the stage in which bacteria do not grow.

    B.   the stage in which bacteria multiply rapidly.

    C.   a one hour period bacteria need to "re-group" and start growing.

    D.   the decline phase of growth.

7.   Food contamination caused by pesticides is called:

    A.   cross contamination.

    B.   physical contamination.

    C.   chemical contamination.

    D.   biological contamination.

8.   What should the manager do about an employee who reports to work with the following symptoms: fever, coughing, and a sore throat?

9.   Why is hand washing so important?

See Appendix E for answers.

CHAPTER 3
HACCP: A Food Protection System

☞ *The Hazard Analysis Critical Control Points (HACCP) system is designed to be used to maximize food safety. HACCP is not a new system. In fact, it was developed in the 1960s to assure that foods prepared for astronauts were safe. HACCP is a simple concept: You identify the hazards and then monitor the critical control points that control the hazards. The canned food industry has kept our food safe by using HACCP for over 20 years.*

The Dangers of Foodborne Illness

U.S. public health officials estimate that foodborne illnesses kill more than 8000 people each year and make millions of people sick. Symptoms range from an upset stomach to serious bloodstream infections. The primary safety hazard with food is not contamination due to pesticides. The biggest problem is **microbiological contamination**. In other words, **microorganisms** of the wrong sort and in excess quantities are the real cause of most foodborne illnesses.

Odd as it may seem, the number of foodborne illness occurrences is on the rise. The factors that contribute to this increase are:

• Changes in eating habits

• New forms of bacterial pathogens

• More consumers with higher vulnerability to disease

• Processed foods that require less cooking

• Longer shipping times

• Additional handling and holding time before foods are served

Types of people who are more vulnerable to foodborne illness include the young, the old, the chronically ill, those with immune problems (such as cancer and AIDS), and people who frequently use antacid medication.

The food service industry works very hard to improve the safety of food. It is important that every food service employee be aware of the potential hazards that exist when serving food to the public.

Safety Assurance through HACCP

The Hazard Analysis Critical Control Points (HACCP) system improves the safety of food by using a logical approach to food safety. Even if HACCP is not required by your local inspectors, it is still an excellent way to teach food safety and produce safe food.

The HACCP concept combines principles of food microbiology, quality control, and risk assessment to obtain, as nearly as possible, a fail-safe system. This approach has been recommended as a method to promote food safety by industry quality assurance personnel, government food safety officials, and international expert committees for over 20 years.

Many public health officials in the United States are encouraging the use of HACCP to shift the emphasis away from the traditional facility-type inspection to one that focuses more on the specific steps that provide safe food.

Traditional inspection programs have focused on sanitation, construction, and appearance. This type of inspection can result in better maintenance, and cleaning of equipment and facilities, but it does not always focus on the specific food handling steps that allow you to produce safe food.

Therefore, a facility could receive a high score on the "traditional" inspection but still have dangerous problems in food handling. As a result, investigations consistently find the same major causes of bacterial illnesses. These are:

- Inadequate food time/temperature control

- Contamination of foods by infected workers, chemicals, equipment, and supplies

Introducing the HACCP System in Your Establishment

For any new system to be successful, everyone must be involved! Developing a HACCP chart is not enough. The users of the program (managers, supervisors, and employees) must understand why, what, and how they need to follow the procedures. HACCP is an organized system that requires planning, implementation, and ongoing evaluation. The following points must be remembered when starting the HACCP system.

1. Education and Motivation   Managers, supervisors, and employees must understand the HACCP system because the program is dependent on the commitment of ALL personnel.

Set up a program to improve the quality and safety of the product. This requires commitment from each employee. Include employees in the process, ask for their input, and **value their contribution.** These actions will foster a sense of pride and personal responsibility. Set up problem-solving groups, ask for individual suggestions, and reward their input. Give the employee a reason to continue in the effort to provide safe food. If you can do this, the program will be a success.

2. The Operation: Facilities, Equipment, and Personnel

The design of the workplace is very important to ensure that foods can flow safely through your facility. You need the right personnel and equipment in the right place to accomplish the goal: safe food!

The HACCP System

The flowchart that follows is from the International Association of Milk, Food, and Environmental Sanitarians, Incorporated, 1991 publication, "Procedures to Implement the Hazard Analysis Critical Control Points System." By knowing the water activity, pH level, temperatures, and times that food is exposed to conditions which are favorable to bacterial growth, and the dangerous microorganisms that could be in the food, problems can be corrected before the food can cause foodborne illness.

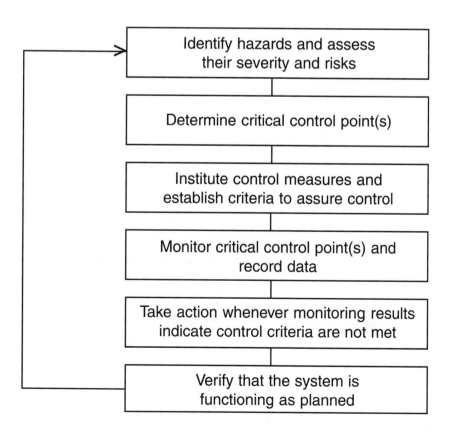

Notes on the flowchart

1. The first step in the HACCP system involves looking at your recipes to identify potentially hazardous foods. Assess the severity of biological, chemical, and physical hazards associated with each step in preparation of the food. Because this step can sometimes be challenging, it can be very helpful to contact an industry, government, or college consultant who has already identified the hazards for different foods.

2. The second step is to determine the critical control points (CCPs), that is, which steps will reduce or eliminate the hazards. These are the steps or points within the process where hazards can best be controlled.

3. The third step is to carry out the HACCP plan, which includes checks and measurements to keep food from becoming contaminated, and the necessary actions to correct problems.

4. The fourth step is to monitor and record each CCP so that you know if the operation is under control.

5. The fifth step is to correct problems when your monitoring procedures show that a CCP is not under control.

6. The final component of the HACCP concept is to verify that the HACCP system is working. This includes reviewing that the appropriate CCPs have been identified for all foods, that CCPs are effectively monitored, and that the appropriate action is taken whenever criteria are not being met. The best way to accomplish this is to have regular meetings to discuss your HACCP system.

Hazards

The "H" of **HACCP** refers to the **hazards** that can cause foodborne illness. These were discussed in Chapter 2. A hazard is unacceptable contamination (biological, chemical, or physical), unacceptable growth, or unacceptable survival of microorganisms that affect safety or spoilage.

This is the first step in developing a HACCP plan. When you are working on a new menu plan, you first need to know what the hazards are before you can determine where the critical control points are.

Foodborne illness investigations have shown the following to be the 10 most frequent hazards.

1. Improper cooling procedures

According to the U.S. Centers for Disease Control, the most common cause of all reported foodborne illnesses is improperly cooling hazardous foods. Improperly cooling allows food to remain in the danger zone (41 to 140°F) and permits rapid bacterial growth that can cause foodborne illness.

The following are some examples of improper cooling.

- Food that is stored in large containers, such as 5-gallon buckets, stockpots, soup kettle inserts, or pans deeper than 4 inches. **These containers are too large! The food in the center of a large container does not cool fast enough to prevent bacterial growth.**

- Hot foods put in containers with tight lids, which slows the cooling process, even when the product is refrigerated.

- Stacking containers of food one on top of the other. This increases the amount of time needed to cool food to 41°F.

- Inadequate cooling units that do not keep the food below 41°F (or below 0°F if frozen).

- Cooler racks which are not arranged in such a way as to allow cold-air circulation all around the surface of storage containers. This prevents products from cooling adequately.

2. Prolonged holding of prepared foods

Foods prepared 12 hours or more before they are served may leave food in the danger zone (between 41 and 140°F) too long.

3. Poor personal hygiene

Handling of food by employees who either have infections and/or use poor personal hygiene transmits foodborne illness through food.

Each supervisor needs to know how an illness is passed from one person to another in food, and what can be done to prevent it from happening.

Personal habits and hand washing are extremely important when handling food!

4. Failure to reheat food rapidly before serving

Using the wrong equipment or not checking the temperature when reheating food are common mistakes that cause many foodborne illnesses. The food must be reheated to 165°F and kept there for the length of time required to kill the microorganisms.

5. Improper hot-holding

The following practices observed during hot-holding will result in contaminated food.

- Foods held warm at temperatures between 70 and 120°F for 4 hours or longer can lead to **tremendous bacterial growth, resulting in outbreaks of food-borne illness or spoilage.**

- Use of hot-holding units for purposes other than those for which they were designed could keep food from the heat source, such as:

    — food displayed in bowls or plates on steam tables; or
    — items stacked on top of each other

- Hot-holding units not operated as intended, such as:

    — thermostats turned lower than recommended or necessary to hold food at 140°F or higher;
    — fans not turned on in units; or
    — glass walls removed from units.

- Mixing new and old food products.

- Time and temperature procedures for reheating and hot-holding not followed correctly.

6. Contaminated raw foods or ingredients

If the food is served raw (such as a salad) and it is cross-contaminated, there will be no opportunity to reduce dangerous microorganisms to safe levels after initial preparation.

7. Use of food from an unapproved source

Food served should never be purchased from an unapproved source. An example of this unsafe practice is when shellfish are harvested from contaminated waters and foodborne illness results. Home-canned foods can be a prime source for botulism. In both instances, these food products should only be purchased from approved sources.

8. Improper cleaning of equipment and utensils

Poor sanitizing procedures, including not cleaning sinks and cutting boards properly, water temperatures below safe levels, or use of weak sanitizing solutions do not reduce the number of bacteria to low levels.

9. Cross-contamination from raw to cooked food

This can occur through:

- Touching a raw food such as chicken or eggs and then, before washing hands, handling a cooked food

- Not separately cleaning any raw food, including fresh vegetables and fruits, which carry soilborne bacteria and not washing hands before touching a cooked food

- Not sanitizing table surfaces, cutting boards, or utensils used to cut seafood, poultry, or raw meat before using for preparing cooked foods causes cross-contamination.

10. Inadequate cooking

This can occur through:

- Undercooking poultry, meats, and seafoods

- Not monitoring internal temperatures when cooking stuffed meats, poultry, and fish

- Not cooking eggs completely

- Not monitoring cooking temperatures of any potentially hazardous food, which could cause a foodborne illness, if undercooked

Another hazardous practice, not listed above but known to cause foodborne illness, is that of using wiping cloths or sponges which have not been rinsed in sanitizing solution after each use.

All of the above are hazards in the food service industry. It is very important to understand and know how to prevent them from occurring in your establishment.

Analysis

The "A" of HACCP stands for **analysis**. When a menu item or a certain preparation procedure is analyzed, a careful study needs to be made of all the parts, or steps, of the process. All menu item recipes can be broken into a list of ingredients, things to do, times, temperatures, etc.

The manager or supervisor usually does not have the scientific equipment, disease surveillance information, or the time to do 2- or 3-day hazard analyses when setting up the HACCP system. Usually, food service industries can supply you with this expertise. However, a knowledge of the following risk factors will help the manager in HACCP analysis.

- **Properties of food.** These include the general water activity (amount of available moisture) and pH values that support or suppress bacterial growth. A list of potentially hazardous foods will be useful in identifying these factors.

- **Food processing/preparation that food will undergo.** Menu item recipes and procedures contain the information about what will be done to prepare the food.

- **Volume of food prepared.** Large quantities of food such as stews, soups, and other multiple-serving menu items require attention to heating, cooling, holding, and reheating procedures. This is due to the density and quantity of the product.

- **Type of customer to be served.** The very old, very young, and persons with immune problems are more susceptible to foodborne illness.

Critical Control Point

The "CCP" in HACCP stands for **critical control points**. A CCP is defined as a point, step, or procedure at which control can be applied and a food safety hazard can be prevented, eliminated, or reduced to acceptable levels. Failure to use the right procedure at any CCP may result in an unacceptable health risk. Points in food preparation that may be CCPs include cooking, chilling, specific sanitation procedures, cross-contamination, and employee hygiene.

Critical control points have to be defined separately for each menu item recipe. The CCPs differ depending on whether the item is to be served hot or cold, whether the ingredients are potentially hazardous, and whether human hands are involved in the preparation.

A step in the process can be a **simple** control point where a biological, physical, or chemical hazard can be controlled. However, a **critical** control point is a step where a hazard can be **prevented, eliminated,** or **reduced** to acceptable levels.

Determining if a step is a CCP is based on the following criteria:

• A preventive measure exists for the hazard.

• The step will eliminate or reduce the likely occurrence of a hazard to an acceptable level, or the step could result in contamination to an unacceptable level and there is no further step to reduce or eliminate the hazard.

• The CCP is a step that can be measured and/or observed.

• Appropriate action can be taken when criteria are not met.

Example: Applying the HACCP System to the Preparation of Fried Chicken

The assessment of the recipe includes the following:

• List the **steps** involved in preparation of the food.

• Determine the **hazards** and **CCPs**.

• Decide the **control/solution** procedures that can be used to provide safe food.

All of these steps and procedures can be put into a complete flowchart to show exactly what is involved in each menu item. We will show the progressive building of a HACCP flowchart in three stages, using fried chicken as an example.

Flowchart Stage 1

The first part of the flowchart consists of the assessment of all the **steps** involved in the flow of the food item. The list for fried chicken might look as follows:

STEP

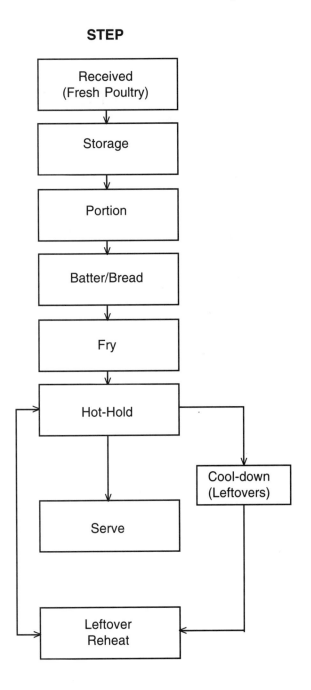

Flowchart Stage 2

In the second part of the assessment the **hazards** associated with the menu item are identified. At the same time the **critical control points** (CCPs) are chosen. The buildup of this sample flowchart may look as follows:

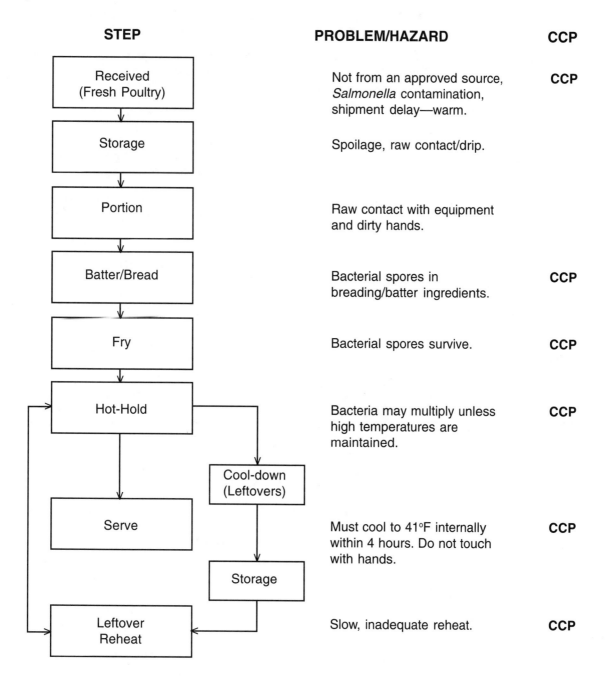

STEP	PROBLEM/HAZARD	CCP
Received (Fresh Poultry)	Not from an approved source, *Salmonella* contamination, shipment delay—warm.	CCP
Storage	Spoilage, raw contact/drip.	
Portion	Raw contact with equipment and dirty hands.	
Batter/Bread	Bacterial spores in breading/batter ingredients.	CCP
Fry	Bacterial spores survive.	CCP
Hot-Hold	Bacteria may multiply unless high temperatures are maintained.	CCP
Cool-down (Leftovers)		
Serve	Must cool to 41°F internally within 4 hours. Do not touch with hands.	CCP
Storage		
Leftover Reheat	Slow, inadequate reheat.	CCP

Flowchart Stage 3

In the last column of the flowchart the **controls** and **solutions** are determined. The example of fried chicken could be done as follows:

STEP	PROBLEM/HAZARD	CCP	CONTROL/SOLUTION
Received (Fresh Poultry)	Not from an approved source, *Salmonella* contamination, shipment delay—warm.	CCP	None practicable. Check incoming shipment. Reject if not below 41°F or not USDA inspected.
Storage	Spoilage, raw contact/drip.		Keep at 41°F or below. Check cooler temperatures. Store below cooked food. Rotate stock on first-in, first-out (FIFO) basis.
Portion	Raw contact with equipment and dirty hands.		Handwashing. Clean/sanitize equipment. Return excess amount to the refrigerator.
Batter/Bread	Bacterial spores in breading/batter ingredients.	CCP	Don't recycle flour or used batter.
Fry	Bacterial spores survive.	CCP	Cook to minimal internal temperature of 165°F. Measure temperature in center of meat.
Hot-Hold	Bacteria may multiply unless high temperatures are maintained.	CCP	Product temperature checks 140°F internal temperature. Measure center of meat every 2 hours. Return to stove and reheat to 165°F.
Cool-down (Leftovers)			
Serve	Must cool to 45°F internally within 4 hours. Do not touch with hands.	CCP	Shallow pans, measure depth. Measure temperature of refrigerator daily. Discard contaminated pieces.
Storage			
Leftover Reheat	Slow, inadequate reheat.	CCP	Reheat to 165°F in less than 2 hours with proper equipment. Measure internal temperature.

Time and Temperature Charting

A sample flowchart worksheet and the monitor worksheet are included in Appendix D for your convenience. The monitor worksheet includes a time/temperature chart. This chart can be used at each stage of the food flow process, from receiving to serving. The key idea of the chart and the most important thing to remember is that foods should not be in the *temperature danger zone* (41 to 140°F) for an extended period of time. This zone is indicated on the chart by heavy black bars. The shaded area of the chart (from 70 to 120°F) is the most dangerous temperature zone. Foods must not remain in this zone for longer than absolutely necessary. This is the temperature range where bacteria multiply most rapidly.

By using the time/temperature chart you will be able to track a menu item and monitor exactly how long the food stayed in the danger zone. When problems are observed on the chart, changes can be made to ensure the production of safe food. After the real and potential problems are known and corrected, spot checks should be sufficient to keep the system going successfully. Sample HACCP forms for your use are provided in Appendix D.

Example: Time/Temperature Charting of Ground Beef

In this exercise, ground beef for casseroles is monitored to determine what actually happened to the product.

In the first example, ground beef was prepared and then accidentally set aside until the end of the day. After cooking, the meat rapidly cooled down to the temperature range of the danger zone and stayed there for at least 12 hours. Since the product should have been kept hot at 140°F or cooled to 41°F within 4 to 6 hours, the possibility for bacterial growth was great. In this situation, *Staphylococcus aureus* grew to unsafe levels.

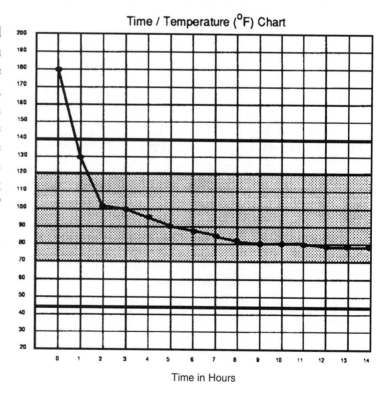

Figure A: Ground beef was kept too long in the danger zone.

In the second example, ground beef was cooked and held hot at 140°F during the time it was in use. Then it was rapidly cooled for storage by using one of the approved methods of cooling. As a result, no significant amounts of harmful bacteria grew in this product. It remained safe to be reheated and used one more time.

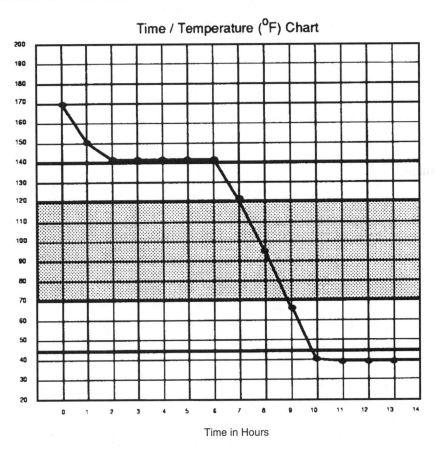

Figure B: Ground beef was handled correctly.

Preplanning Menu Items

Planning how much food to prepare is always a challenge. Each manager or supervisor must decide what the menu item needs are for a given time or day. However, and this is even more important, after the food has been prepared, it must be kept out of the danger zone. You need to decide whether it is more cost-effective to properly cool a product and reheat it later, or simply to throw it out. The responsibility for keeping food safe and controlling the "bottom line" is the job of the manager.

The HACCP system can provide you with the information needed to make safe and rational decisions about food resource management.

Use the HACCP system as a helper!

Summary

The HACCP process provides a model for analyzing and identifying the critical control points, based on the particular hazards that are part of every menu item recipe.

The use of the Hazard Analysis Critical Control Points (HACCP) system emphasizes the ever-present possibility of the growth of microorganisms. Determining the right actions at specific times and avoiding the wrong ones are important factors for protecting both the food and your customers.

There are several ways in which food can become contaminated. Poorly cleaned utensils, equipment, and surfaces are common places for contaminants to enter the food. Improper cooling and reheating are practices which allow food contaminants to survive and grow to harmful levels. And last, but not least, the people who prepare and serve the food are always potential sources of contamination in the food service industry. Knowing what to look for, and how to protect the food, lowers the risk of foodborne illness.

Chapter 3 Review Questions

1.   What do the letters "HACCP" stand for?

2.   List at least six of the most serious hazards in preparing food:

      A.

      B.

      C.

      D.

      E.

      F.

3.   Explain what a critical control point (CCP) is:

See Appendix E for answers.

CHAPTER 4
Purchasing, Receiving, and Storing Food

☞ *All foods accepted into a food service establishment must be carefully inspected and correctly stored to ensure their highest quality and to protect them from contamination and deterioration. Implementation of any HACCP or safety assurance program begins with purchasing, receiving, and storing.*

Food Suppliers

Approved Sources

Food products used in food service establishments must be obtained from reliable sources. Choose suppliers who are known to sell clean, fresh, uncontaminated food products. Whenever possible, tour the facility of the suppliers. Food processing plants with quality assurance and/or HACCP programs in place can supply verification of procedures used to protect products and have been approved by the appropriate regulatory agency. **Food prepared in a private home must not be used or offered for sale in a food service establishment.**

State and federal agencies regulate the safety of food products. Check the regulations in your state for details (for additional information, see Chapter 11).

Inspecting Merchandise

Incoming shipments of food must be inspected for spoilage and other contamination. All employees receiving food shipments should be trained to know and use the following guidelines. When possible, have deliveries scheduled during slow periods of business so that food products can be examined carefully and quickly moved to their proper storage areas.

- Check the condition of the delivery truck to determine how the food was protected during shipping. Look for signs of mud, dirt, water, oil stains, bad odors, or lack of cleaning and sanitizing between shipments. Non-food items should not be included in shipments with food products.

Inspect incoming foods for purchase specifications and quality.

- Check temperatures of the food received in refrigerated shipments to be sure that chilled products are at or below 41°F, and frozen products are below a temperature of 0°F. Hot foods should be at 140°F or above.

- Reject packages that are damaged, patched, or taped shut. If cartons and containers in the shipment are broken, crushed, or otherwise damaged, their contents may be contaminated and should be rejected.

- Examine the contents of some foods for contamination and food quality. A random sample will help you spot unacceptable food products.

- Check for contamination between raw and prepared food products during shipping. Raw and prepared food products should be covered carefully and stored separately.

- Foods should not contain unapproved additives or levels that exceed allowable amounts.

- Reject any shipment that is not up to standards. Safety assurance of safety using HACCP begins with purchasing and receiving.

Note: Company policy often determines how the rejected materials are to be returned. Check for procedures.

Thermometers

Thermometers must be used to check the temperatures of incoming shipments of food products, final cooking temperatures, food temperatures in refrigerators, freezers, and hot-holding units. They are also used to monitor the temperatures of solutions used for cleaning and sanitizing.

- Never use glass or mercury-filled thermometers; they could break and contaminate food. Use only bimetallic stemmed thermometers for checking food temperatures.

- Use thermometers that are at least 5 inches long. Insert the lower 2 inches into food to take a reading. Do not touch the bottom or sides of the containers with the thermometer.

- Do not leave the bimetallic thermometer with the plastic lens cover on the gauge in food being cooked; it could melt and contaminate the food.

- Digital thermometers also are available in a variety of styles and are calibrated according to manufacturers' directions.

- Use thermometers that can measure food temperatures ranging from 0 to 220°F without freezing or breaking. They must be accurate to within plus or minus 2°F.

- Check the accuracy of thermometers regularly. Use water and ice slush in a cup and adjust to a 32°F reading, or place in a pan of boiling water and adjust when the indicator stops rising to 212°F. Calibrate thermometers routinely and see manufacturers' directions, if necessary. At high elevations, adjustments may have to be made.

- Clean and sanitize thermometers after each use. Use a sanitizer approved for food contact surfaces. Clean and sanitize thermometer cases on a regular basis.

- Monitor temperatures using thermometers mounted in equipment. Check thermometers' accuracy by comparing to the bimetallic stemmed thermometer. All thermometers should be checked for accuracy on a routine basis.

Receiving Fresh Foods

Meat

Meat and meat products must be inspected by a federal or state regulatory program which checks the safety of the product and sanitary conditions of the processing plant. Meat carcasses that pass USDA inspection bear a circular stamp identifying the plant where the meat was processed. The circular stamp is for safety and wholesomeness of the product. This is a mandatory inspection stamp. Grading stamps for quality are not required; however, meat that has been graded for quality should be purchased. You may ask suppliers for written confirmation that individual cuts of meat have been officially inspected.

Meats that pass USDA inspection bear a circular identification stamp.

It is the responsibility of the manager to check with suppliers if any discrepancies or unusual problems are found in a shipment.

- When receiving meat, check all packaging. Dirty, torn, damaged, or broken wrapping and boxes may mean that the meat is contaminated and should be rejected.

- Check the internal temperature of fresh meat and reject cuts that are warmer than 41°F (or the temperature required in your area).

- Check that meats are light pink to red and uniform in color. Aged beef may be darker in color.

- Check all fresh meats for smell and reject them if there is a sour or rancid odor.

- Check that the texture of fresh meat is firm and elastic. Any meat that feels slimy, sticky, or dry should be rejected. Frozen meats should be 0°F or below and show no signs of defrosting or refreezing upon delivery.

- Check for a USDA inspection stamp for safety and wholesomeness, which is mandatory for meats.

Do not buy meat from an unknown source.

Buy inspected meat.

- Check packages of ground meat with extra care because it spoils quicker than does intact muscle tissue. Highly processed products are more likely to be contaminated, due to exposure to air, equipment, and humans.

Sausages with evidence of slime or mold should be rejected, except for dry sausages such as salami or pepperoni. The mold that forms on their exterior casing is not dangerous but should be removed.

Poultry

Poultry and poultry meat products, including game birds, must be inspected officially under a federal or state regulatory program.

- Use only Grade A poultry. Inspection information and the producer's identification must appear on labels on the containers in which poultry products are received.

- The receiving temperature of the meat must be **below** 41°F. When delivered and stored, fresh poultry should be packed in crushed ice.

- Reject poultry that has a purple or greenish color. Other signs of spoilage include an abnormal or bad smell, darkened wing tips, and soft, flabby, or sticky flesh. A high percentage of poultry will be contaminated with *Salmonella*. Handle carefully to avoid cross-contamination.

Seafood

Know your suppliers. Buy fish from vendors who follow state and federal guidelines. Be sure that the fish was caught in safe, unpolluted waters and that it is fresh.

- Fresh fish should be delivered and stored packed in crushed ice and should have a receiving temperature between 32 and 41°F.

- Acceptable fresh fish has bright skin, with gills that are moist and red and scales firmly attached. The eyes must be clear and bulging.

- The flesh should be firm and elastic when touched and should not separate easily from the bone.

- Fish that have a strong odor, soft flesh, discolored or dry gills, or eyes that are cloudy, red-rimmed, and sunken are not acceptable and should be rejected. Also, look for signs of worms, diseases, and tumors.

- Crustaceans and shellfish must come from approved sources. Only shellfish from approved waters can be sold. The harvesting, tagging, handling, shipping, and marketing of shellfish must follow regulatory standards as described in the FDA's National Shellfish Sanitation Program Manual of Operations. Identification tags must be dated on receipt and held for 90 days. Companies that supply you with molluscan shellfish should be listed in FDA's Interstate Certified Shellfish Shippers List.

- Fresh shellfish should be alive when they are delivered and should not have a strong odor. The shells of live clams and oysters should be closed or should close when tapped. Shucked shellfish should be kept in the original container until used. This means that even if there is only one dozen in the 12-dozen box, the original container must be kept.

Milk and Dairy Products

- All milk and dairy products used in food service establishments must be pasteurized.

- Milk with a receiving temperature above 41°F must be rejected unless otherwise specified by local laws.

- The expiration date on the package gives the last date that a milk product may be sold. Any packages after that date should be rejected.

- Reject milk that does not contain the standards established for odor, taste, and appearance that you require.

- All fluid milk and fluid milk products must be grade A pasteurized and clearly marked with the name of the processor. Expiration dates must be visible and should be checked when the milk is delivered.

- Milk that is served as a beverage should be taken from the container the milk was packaged in at the milk plant. Once milk is taken from the original container it must not be put back in the container or reused in any way. When a bulk dispenser is not available and portions of less than one-half pint are required, a commercial container of not more than one-half gallon is used to remove the smaller portions.

- Individual fluid creamers must be stored at 41°F or less. Products labeled UHT (ultrahigh temperature) are sterile and do not require refrigeration until opened. Dry milk products must be reconstituted with potable water in a clean sanitary container and kept at temperatures at or below 41°F until used.

- Butter should have a firm texture and even color with no signs of mold or rancid smell. Containers should be clean and unbroken.

- Cheese should have a uniform color and texture, and should be rejected if it is discolored, excessively moldy, or dried out. Cheeses with rinds should be clean and undamaged.

- Bakery products with custard or cream fillings require careful handling and should always be transported and stored at 41°F or below.

Eggs

- Fresh eggs should be refrigerated immediately upon delivery. Since damaged eggs may be contaminated with bacteria, check the shells for cracks and dirt. You may check the freshness and temperature of a shipment of eggs by breaking one or two open and measuring the temperature with a metal stemmed thermometer.

- Acceptable eggs will have no noticeable odor, the yolk will be firm, and the white will cling to the yolk and temperature will be below 41°F, unless otherwise specified by local laws.

- Liquid, frozen, and dry eggs must be pasteurized.

Fruits and Vegetables

The best indication of quality in fruits and vegetables is taste; however, fresh fruits and vegetables spoil easily when not handled carefully.

- Slightly blemished produce can be acceptable if flavor and quality are not affected.

- All produce must be thoroughly washed in potable water before serving. This reduces possible contamination by soilborne bacteria or chemical residue from pesticides. Blemished areas should be cut away and discarded.

Receiving Processed Foods

Frozen Foods

- Ice for use as a food or for cooling other foods must be made from drinking water.

- Frozen food products should be checked for signs of deterioration, especially for signs of thawing and refreezing.

- Do not accept delivery of frozen foods if you find fluid or frozen liquids in the carton or if the product contains large ice crystals.

- Frozen foods should have an internal temperature of 0°F or below.

- Check the temperature of frozen foods with a sanitized stainless steel thermometer. Insert the thermometer between the packages and leave until the reading stabilizes.

- Do not accept foods that have been thawed and refrozen. Ice in the bottom of a carton, large ice crystals, or a deformed container indicate that thawing and refreezing have taken place.

- Reject any packages that are not sealed tightly.

Refrigerated Foods

- All shipments of refrigerated foods should be inspected immediately and must be moved into coolers as soon as they arrive. The temperature must be kept at 41°F or below as required by the product.

- If the packaging is damaged, or if there are any signs of contamination, do not accept the shipment.

Packaged Foods

- All packaged foods you buy, including those in airtight, heat-sealed containers, must be processed and packaged in an approved commercial food processing plant.

- Be sure that all processed egg products, including frozen or dehydrated eggs, are pasteurized and purchased from plants operating under continuous inspection.

Modified-Atmosphere Packaging

Modified-atmosphere packaging is the term used to describe food processing methods where food is packed using a system that withdraws all air from the package. Gases can be added after the air is removed, to aid in preserving food. Food that is vacuum packed can maintain flavor and extend shelf life as long as it is handled properly. Vacuum-packed foods must be kept at temperatures of 41°F or below and used within the time indicated on the package.

Check with your local or state health department before attempting modified-atmosphere packaging, as there may be additional requirements before you are allowed to do this procedure in your facility.

Vacuum-packed fish must be stored at temperatures of 38°F or below. Because oxygen is removed from products, *C. botulinum* can grow if temperatures are not kept enough below 41°F to suppress bacterial growth.

When the product is packaged and labeled **sous vide**, the food is vacuum packed and **then** fully or partly cooked. The packages are stored at temperatures of 32 to 38°F until used. The FDA allows only certified establishments to produce sous vide products, and managers must purchase from these approved sources. Processing plants must provide proof of FDA approval and have an approved HACCP plan. Teach your employees the dangers of mishandling vacuum-packed foods. Follow manufacturers' directions on storing and cooking.

Check vacuum-packaged foods for temperature and for damaged packaging. Some vacuum-packed foods have a special label that contains liquid crystals that change color permanently when the item has reached an unsafe temperature level. This time/temperature indicator (TTI) also is used on sous vide and modified-atmosphere packaging products. Always follow the processor's instructions for handling and storing vacuum-packed foods.

Canned Foods

Botulism can occur in canned and vacuum-packed foods and is extremely dangerous. All canned goods must be checked thoroughly when received and again just before you use them.

- Check for leakage, broken seals, dents along seams, rust, or missing labels.

- Examine both ends and seams of a can and press each end separately. If the opposite end bulges or the pressed end springs back, the can should be rejected.

- If any of these conditions are detected, reject the canned product.

Dry Foods

Dry foods include such products as cereals, sugars, flour, and dried fruits and vegetables. Check for signs of contamination and reject any products that appear to be damaged.

- Be sure these foods are completely dry when received. Check for dampness or molds. Even small amounts of moisture can promote rapid and dangerous bacterial growth.

- Look for punctures, tears, holes, or slashes in the packaging that may indicate the presence of insects or rodents.

- Check that the boxes are clean and undamaged.

Storing Food and Supplies

Protecting Stored Food

Proper storage is necessary to preserve the quality of food and to prevent contamination and spoilage. The following information can be critical to the safety of the food and customers in your establishment.

FIFO

The most important rule of storage is *first in, first out*, (FIFO). This means that food products should be used in the order in which they are received. Date foods as they are received to keep track. Place new deliveries of food behind the older stock in storage areas to be sure that the older food products are used first.

Containers

Whenever possible, store foods in their original packaging. If food is removed from its original packaging, take special care in repacking for storage. Prevent contamination by keeping food covered in clean, nonabsorbent containers until it is prepared and served. Clearly label repackaged foods—especially food such as cooking oil, syrup, salt, sugar, or flour—that are not stored in their original containers. Be especially careful that chemical and food products are labeled correctly and stored separately.

Metal containers may cause contamination when certain foods come in contact with them. Foods that have a high acid content, such as fruit products, lemonade, sauerkraut, and tomatoes, react strongly with metals. Avoid using containers made of copper, brass, tin, or galvanized metal. Enamelware can be dangerous if plated with antimony or cadmium. Equipment containing these metals must be avoided in all phases of food preparation, storage, and service.

Placement

To prevent cross-contamination, different types of raw animal products, such as beef, fish, lamb, pork, or poultry, should be separated from each other during storage. Keep them in separate containers so that they cannot come in contact with each other. Be sure to prevent food from dripping on other food products. Raw food products should be separated from ready-to-eat food products by storing the raw products below the ready-to-eat products. **Always store raw meat, poultry, and fish away from or below all other foods.**

Store food products at a minimum of 6 inches above the floor on clean shelves, racks, dollies, or other surfaces. Do not store food or containers of food under exposed or unprotected water or sewage lines. Pipes can drip moisture and contaminate the food.

Contamination

Store food only in designated areas, NEVER in passageways, rest rooms, dressing rooms, garbage rooms, utility rooms, or under other sources of contamination.

Protect food from dust, flies, rodents, and other pests, toxic materials, unclean equipment and utensils, unnecessary handling, coughs and sneezes, and all other sources of contamination. During storage, protect from cross-contamination by contact with other foods all food that will not be washed or cooked before serving.

Refrigerated Foods

Refrigerator temperatures should be kept **below** 41°F. Refrigerators with temperatures of 41°F could have difficulty maintaining 41°F food temperatures. Place thermometers in several areas of the refrigerator where they can easily be read and checked often. Remember, thermometers must be **visible and accurate.** Check the **internal** temperatures of refrigerated foods on a regular basis, to make sure that the foods are kept at 41°F or less. If only one thermometer is used in the refrigerator, place it in the warmest part of the unit. Thermometers should be checked regularly to be sure that they are accurate.

- Always refrigerate fresh meat, poultry, and fish.

- Cover stored foods to prevent contamination from other products or direct contact with refrigerator shelves that contain cadmium. Sides and quarters of meat may be hung uncovered on clean sanitized hooks if no food product is stored beneath the meat.

- Fresh fish should be stored in crushed ice and kept drained.

- Most fruits and vegetables are kept best refrigerated and should not be washed before refrigeration. Uncooked produce that does NOT require refrigeration includes apples, pears, bananas, avocados, citrus fruits, onions, potatoes, and eggplants. This produce keeps best at room temperature. For apples, pears, bananas, and avocados that are not ripe, ripen at room temperature and then refrigerate to maintain quality.

- If possible, provide separate units with different temperatures for different types of foods. If different foods must be stored in the same unit, store meats, fish, and dairy foods in the coldest part.

- To prevent cross-contamination, be sure that prepared foods are stored above raw foods.

Do not store any food, especially packaged food and wrapped sandwiches, where they can get wet.

- Do not overload refrigerators. Too much food in the unit can raise the temperature of the entire unit. Have enough conveniently located refrigeration facilities to keep potentially hazardous foods at required temperatures during storage.

- All stored foods must be kept covered at all times. The one exception is when warm foods are being cooled to 41°F, in which case a partial covering allows the product to cool faster. Cover completely after 41°F is reached.

- Do not store refrigerated foods on the floor of a walk-in refrigerator. All food products must be stored on shelves at least 6 inches above the floor.

- Food packages should be stored in such a way that cold air can circulate around all surfaces of the container.

Frozen Foods

Keep the temperature range for frozen foods between 0 and –10°F. Check thermometers on a regular basis.

- Do not thaw and refreeze frozen foods.

- Do not thaw food at room temperature.

- Keep frozen foods in moistureproof packaging.

- Use the FIFO (first in, first out) rule.

- Store frozen foods to allow for air circulation between the packages.

- Do not freeze large quantities of unfrozen foods. This can raise the temperature of the entire unit and damage stored foods.

- Defrost freezers regularly. This helps maintain a proper airflow for better performance. During defrosting, use food immediately or move it to another freezer before thawing occurs.

- Be sure that foods do not thaw during the defrost cycle of self-defrosting freezers.

Dry Foods

Apply the FIFO rule to dry food storage as well. Even canned foods do not last forever and should be used as soon as possible.

- Keep foods in dry storage tightly covered and protected from contamination.

- Remember that cereals and pasta can deteriorate rapidly if exposed to moisture.

- Wipe cans with a clean cloth before they are opened and used.

Because moisture in foods such as cereal, flour, and rice causes deterioration and spoilage, dry storage areas must be designed and maintained to keep humidity levels low.

- Keep these areas well ventilated and well lighted.

- Store foods at least 6 inches off the floor in a way that allows adequate air circulation.

- Store items on ventilated shelves.

- Install window coverings or frosted glass to reduce heat and exposure to light.

- Cover all interior surfaces with easy-to-clean, corrosion-resistant materials.

Contamination is spread by poor storage practices.

- Protect dry foods from dripping condensation or leakage from overhead plumbing pipes.

- Do not allow smoking, eating, or drinking in dry storage areas. Check with local health department for specific rules.

- Do not store garbage in dry storage areas.

- Seal walls and baseboards to help keep out pests. Keeping the area clean and well maintained will discourage pests.

Both moisture and temperature are factors that can cause food to spoil rapidly. The higher the humidity or the higher the temperature, the faster food spoils. Lowering either one or both of these to acceptable levels will increase the shelf life of food. Furthermore, moist and warm conditions will promote insect growth and reproduction.

The best temperature for dry storage areas is 50°F. A temperature of 50°F can increase the shelf life of most dry products. Humidity levels must also be monitored in dry food storage areas. A relative humidity of 50 to 60% is satisfactory for storing most goods.

Modified-Atmosphere Packaged Foods

Vacuum packaging and sous vide products must be stored under refrigeration according to manufacturers' instructions. Expiration dates must be checked and products used within the suggested safe time limits.

Storing Supplies

Poisonous materials are prohibited in most areas of a food service establishment. Only toxic materials that are required for sanitizing, cleaning, and pest control may be present near food preparation operations. Toxic materials must be labeled, stored, and used only in ways that will not contaminate food. Insecticides and rodenticides must not be used in any way that contaminates food, utensils, or equipment. Sanitizing and cleaning compounds that are nontoxic in dilution must be kept in properly labeled containers.

To prevent contamination, poisonous and toxic materials must be stored below food, equipment, utensils, and single-service articles, or completely separated by a solid partition.

Pesticides must be physically separated from other cleaners, sanitizers, and toxic materials. All chemicals must be stored in properly labeled containers. Pesticides and poisons should be stored in a locked cabinet or area away from food storage areas. Expiration dates of chemicals and pesticides should be monitored. When expired, they should be disposed of safely and immediately.

Summary

Purchasing, receiving, and storing food are the first steps in the management of food products on their way to the customer's table. Using the right methods to purchase, receive, and store food helps ensure that you will have safe products to use.

Chapter 4 Review Questions

1. Can brownies or cookies made in a private home be served/sold in your food service establishment?

2. Name at least five things to check when receiving food items:

    A.

    B.

    C.

    D.

    E.

3. What are the proper receiving and storing temperatures for:

    A.   Frozen foods?

    B.   Refrigerated foods?

4. What do the letters FIFO stand for, and what does the phrase mean?

5. Where in the refrigerator must thawing meat be placed?

6. Shellfish sold in a food establishment must be

    A.   washed before cooking

    B.   removed from the original container

    C.   purchased from a certified packer

    D.   frozen

7. Before accepting delivery of food shipments, employees should

    A.   refreeze any foods that have thawed

    B.   check for signs of rodent and insect activity

C.   trust the delivery person

D.   not open cartons

8.   All milk and milk products used in food establishments

A.   must be in bulk containers

B.   must be ultrapasteurized

C.   should be delivered warmer than 41°F

D.   must be rated Grade A

9.   The best temperature for dry storage areas is

A.   32°F

B.   41°F

C.   50°F

D.   80°F

See Appendix E for answers.

CHAPTER 5
Preparing and Serving Food

☞ *Careful preparation is the key to serving safe food. This includes temperature control and strict compliance with sanitary procedures for cooking, cooling, reheating, holding, and serving foods. The HACCP system focuses attention on the problems that can occur during preparation and serving so that errors can be corrected before contaminated food reaches the consumer.*

Preparing and Serving Food

Throughout the period of preparation and service, food is at highest risk for contamination. Employees must be taught how to minimize the risk of contaminating the food during this time. Through all stages of food preparation and service, monitor:

• Employee health, personal hygiene, and hand washing

• Proper time and temperature control of food

• Cleaning and sanitizing of utensils, equipment, and all food contact surfaces

Employee Health, Personal Hygiene, and Hand Washing

The importance of employee personal hygiene and hand washing was discussed in Chapter 2. It is in the area of food preparation and service that the reason for the emphasis on health, personal hygiene, and hand washing should become very clear to you. Humans provide an ideal environment for the growth of microorganisms. Since prevention is the best way to avoid foodborne illness, the first step is employee health and hygiene. A few simple rules that must be enforced by the food manager are absolutely necessary in the effort to serve safe food.

Except for washing fruits and vegetables, food employees should not touch ready-to-eat foods with their bare hands, and should use clean gloves, deli tissue, spatulas, or tongs.

Time and Temperature Control

Any time that food temperatures are in the danger zone, bacterial growth can occur. The **danger zone** is the range between **41 and 140°F**. Check with local authorities for any variation in the danger zone range because some jurisdictions may use different temperatures, such as 45 to 140°F or 41 to 150°F.

The range between 70 and 140°F is especially dangerous because microorganisms grow rapidly when the food is this warm. Even when the food is going to be cooked using temperatures hot enough to kill the microorganisms present, if a toxin has been produced that is not sensitive to heat, the food will be contaminated.

Although the manager is always responsible for everything in the facility, all personnel must understand and use time/temperature control procedures. Use accurate thermometers and monitor the temperatures and amount of time that food is kept at various stages of preparation and service. The HACCP system includes strict attention to time and temperature.

Most menu items have a specific time and temperature requirement for cooking. Insert the thermometer in different areas of the product, especially the thickest part. Remember — the temperature of the equipment (stove, oven, steam table, etc.) is not the best temperature to check. Monitoring the internal temperature of the product is the **ONLY WAY** to make sure that food has been heated thoroughly to the correct internal temperature.

Storing Ready-to-Eat, Potentially Hazardous Foods

Refrigerated, ready-to-eat, potentially hazardous foods should be discarded if not sold within 10 days.

Cleaning and Sanitizing

Cleaning and sanitizing are covered in Chapter 7.

Destroying Parasites

Although rare, some foodborne illness is caused by parasites in fish. To kill the parasites, raw, marinated, or lightly cooked fish (except molluscan shellfish) must be frozen at −4°F or below for 7 days in a freezer, or at −31°F for 15 hours in a blast freezer.

Thawing Food

Frozen foods must be thawed carefully to prevent contamination and spoilage. **NEVER THAW FOOD AT ROOM TEMPERATURE.** Frozen food should be thawed:

- Under refrigeration with the temperature of the food remaining below 41°F and the product used as soon as possible after it thaws

- By cooking frozen food on the stove or in an oven as a continuous (freezer to stove or oven) process

- In a microwave oven, either to thaw and move to a conventional cooking stove/ oven, or to cook completely

- Under potable running water at a water temperature of 70°F or below with a good water flow for a period of time that does not allow thawed parts to be above 41°F for more than 4 hours

Preparation of Menu Items

When menu items are being prepared, foods are handled in a variety of ways. During the time that foods are being washed, peeled, chopped, mixed, or otherwise being prepared, there are many opportunities for the food to become contaminated.

The principles of **cross-contamination** that were covered in Chapter 2 are very important during this stage of preparation. Raw and cooked product must be kept separate and food contact surfaces that have touched raw food must be cleaned and sanitized before a cooked food touches the same surface.

The amount of time that a food is out of refrigeration is extremely important. Begin the cooking process immediately or refrigerate food if it is to be cooked at a later time. Chill ingredients before they are used in cold foods. Keep to a minimum the time a food is held in the danger zone. These actions will add to the quality and safety of the final product.

Additives

You must not apply sulfiting agents to fresh fruits and vegetables.

Be sure not to accidentally contaminate foods with unapproved food and color additives, or unsafe levels of any additives.

Cooking Food

Always cook foods using the proper equipment. Recipes specify cooking at a certain temperature for a certain amount of time. To be sure that harmful bacteria are killed, foods must be brought to the required temperatures inside as well as outside. Using a thermometer, check internal temperatures and serving temperatures of the foods.

Check internal temperatures in more than one place when heating foods. An acceptable temperature in one spot does not mean that every part of the food has reached the required internal temperature.

For food that is being chilled, check temperatures in the same way as for cooked food. Measure temperatures in the center or the thickest part of the food and in other places as well.

Thermometers

Use only thermometers with stainless steel stems. Glass and mercury-filled thermometers can easily break and contaminate foods.

Use thermometers that are easy to read, with a numerical scale, and accurate within plus or minus 2°F. Check the accuracy of thermometers regularly, in either a pan of boiling water or a cup of slushy ice and water.

Take readings only after the indicator stops moving.

Clean and sanitize the thermometer with alcohol or a sanitizer between uses and let it return to room temperature before using it again.

Cooking Temperatures for Meats

The lowest temperatures that can be used to cook many foods are regulated by law, especially for meat. The best way to kill bacteria in potentially hazardous food is by heating the food to an internal temperature of 165°F and holding it at 140°F or above.

The FDA Food Code provides more flexibility than did previous regulations. Different cooking temperatures and times are available for certain foods.

With the exception of rare roast beef and pasteurized eggs, raw animal foods such as eggs, fish, poultry, and meat must be cooked to at least an internal temperature of 145°F or above for 15 seconds.

Pork, pork products, game animals, chopped fish and meats, and eggs not immediately served must be cooked until heated to an internal temperature of at least 155°F for 15 seconds, 150°F for 1 minute, or 145°F for 3 minutes.

Poultry, meat, and seafoods that contain stuffing, and stuffing containing fish, meat, or poultry, should be cooked to an internal temperature of 165°F.

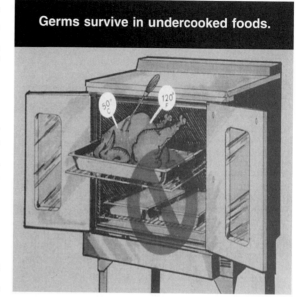

Germs survive in undercooked foods.

Beef roasts and corned beef must be cooked to a minimum internal temperature of 130°F in 121 minutes. Cooking time and methods must ensure that even a large roast, to be served rare, will reach that temperature throughout.

The recommended temperature for ground beef is 155°F for 15 seconds. Steak tartare, which is served raw, is an exception. For this dish, use only fresh beef, minimize handling, and keep it chilled at or below 41°F until serving.

Always measure internal temperatures in more than one place in the food to determine if meat is cooked to the desired temperature.

Breaded or battered meats must be cooked thoroughly. Check temperatures of oil or shortening and monitor the time required for cooking. Discard unused batter and breading mixtures—do not hold over for the next day. Raw product contamination and spores in breading prevent reuse of batters and breading.

Microwave Cooking

For microwave cooking of raw animal foods, you **must**:

*   Rotate or stir the food throughout, or at least midway, in the cooking process.

*   Cook the food to a safe internal temperature that is 25°F above the temperature for oven heating.

- Check with local authorities on whether microwave cooking of pork is allowed.

- Allow the microwaved food to stand covered for 2 minutes after cooking.

Serving Food

Although rare, certain foods (such as raw, marinated fish; raw shellfish; steak tartare; or a partially cooked food such as lightly cooked fish, rare meat, and soft-cooked eggs) have a greater chance than others of causing a foodborne illness. These include raw and undercooked meats, poultry, and seafoods. The FDA Food Code states that customers should be informed that they are taking a greater risk with these raw or undercooked foods. Although this is a controversial proposal, it is one way that you might reduce the impact of liability.

Therefore, before you serve food, you must consider who your customers are. People who are highly susceptible to foodborne illnesses, such as the elderly, persons being served in healthcare settings, and preschool children, should not be served raw or undercooked foods that could make them seriously ill.

Your regulatory authority can grant you a variance in some of these cooking times and temperatures if you have an **approved HACCP** plan (Chapter 3) and information showing that less time and temperature will result in safe food.

It is always best to check with your local health department for the exact temperatures specific to your area.

Food Display

Food on display must be protected from contamination by use of packaging; counter, service line, or salad bar food guards; display cases; or other effective means.

Holding Heated Food

During the time between cooking and serving, hot foods should be stored in equipment that keeps them at the required temperature above 140°F at all times. Holding equipment includes steam trays or tables, steam kettles, heat lamps, and insulated food transport carriers. All holding equipment must be able to maintain a temperature above 140°F. **Never use holding equipment for heating foods.** Holding equipment heats too slowly to be effective and leaves potentially hazardous foods in the danger zone too long, allowing bacteria to multiply to a dangerous level.

Because holding devices provide irregular heat, a food thermometer must be used to check that the food stays at the proper temperature. Each holding device should be equipped with an easy-to-read, numerically scaled thermometer that is accurate to within 3°F either way (or a metal stemmed thermometer must be available).

Avoid holding heated food for long periods of time; it may lose its quality. In addition, the longer the food is held, the greater the chance of it becoming contaminated.

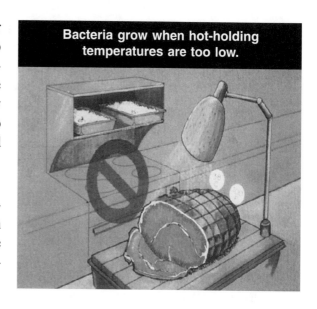

Bacteria grow when hot-holding temperatures are too low.

Stir foods to make certain that they remain hot throughout.

Cover containers to retain heat and protect food against splash, spillage, and contaminants.

When proper holding temperatures are not maintained, foodborne bacteria can grow rapidly to dangerous levels. Check the temperatures frequently with a metal stemmed thermometer. Set out smaller portions to make it easier to maintain temperatures. When following the HACCP system, record temperatures of food being monitored on a temperature graph or make a quick notation to be used in evaluating the safeness of the product. When possible, use batch cooking. Cooking small portions of the food frequently will eliminate holding food for long periods of time.

Bacteria grow when cooked foods are left at room temperature.

Milk Products

Milk and milk products must be kept fresh and sanitary and served in a way that prevents contamination. Only pasteurized milk and milk products may be used.

- Keep all dairy products at 41°F or below for serving.

- Milk must be served from the container in which it was packaged at the milk plant.

Cream, half-and-half, and nondairy creaming and whitening products should be served in individual, unopened containers, protected pour-type pitchers, or drawn from a refrigerated dispenser designed for such service. The factors of time and temperature control **always** apply. If the product is marked UHT, it will not need to be refrigerated until it is opened.

Dry milk and dry milk products may be used in instant desserts and whipped products or for cooking and baking purposes. When these products are reconstituted, they must be stored in sanitized, covered containers at 41°F or below.

When ice cream is dispensed from a bulk pack, it should be served with a scoop located in a dipper well with running water, in the food with the handle extending out of the pack, or clean and dry. Self-service of hard ice cream is not permitted.

When butter or margarine is given to customers for self-service, it should be provided in individual servings.

Unwrapped foods, once served to the customer, may not be re-served or reused; it must be thrown away. For example, bread or rolls, chips, salsa, or large butter pads cannot be re-served or reused and must be thrown away.

Eggs and Egg Products

Recent outbreaks of salmonellosis traced to shell eggs have caused much concern among public health officials. Federal recommendations state that since eggs are potentially haz-ardous foods, they are to be transported, received, and stored at temperatures below 41°F.

All raw egg products in Caesar salad, hollandaise or bernaise sauce, noncommercial mayon-naise, eggnog, ice cream, egg-fortified beverages, or other recipes requiring little or no cooking should be pasteurized, either by jurisdictional law or common practice. Holding tempera-tures on cooked eggs must be 145°F or above for 15 seconds. The same care in cooking, holding, and serving any other potentially hazardous food must be used with eggs and egg products to prevent foodborne illness.

Pasteurized eggs are especially important to use if you have highly susceptible customers. Use pasteurized eggs when they are broken, stored in a container and not immediately served, or when cooked eggs are held before serving.

Beverages and Ice

Ice used as a food or for cooling must be from approved sources (such as drinking water) and must be protected from contamination.

- Ice used to cool down food for storage, food containers, or food utensils cannot be served to people. This ice must be separate from ice used for consumption.

- Cover ice containers between uses and clean and sanitize them regularly. Make sure that ice storage bins are well drained and there is an air gap to prevent backflow.

- Dispense ice only with scoops, tongs, or other suitable equipment. **Do not use** hands, cups, or glasses to scoop ice. Store ice-dispensing utensils that are not in use on a clean surface or in the ice with the handle extending out of the ice or in ice scoop holders that are clean, dry, and self-draining.

- The handle of the scoop should never touch the ice and your hands should never touch the surface of the ice.

- Handle ice as carefully as you would handle food.

Handling Tableware and Utensils

All tableware and serving utensils must be handled in a careful, sanitary way, before, during, and after serving food, to minimize contamination. **Do not** touch the eating surfaces of tableware when setting tables, handling, and storing utensils. Be especially careful not to touch eating surfaces when clearing or bussing tables.

- Hold plates by the bottom or at the edge. Hold cups by the handle or the bottom. Hold knives, forks, and spoons by the handle. Never touch food contact surfaces with your hands.

- When storing flatware in drawers or holders, place them so that they can be picked up by their handles. Store all flatware running in the same direction to protect food contact surfaces from human contact.

- Never carry glasses or cups by putting your fingers inside the glass or by the rim.

- Use a self-draining bar mat to store glasses upside down.

- Wash hands between handling dirty and clean tableware and utensils.

Avoid unnecessary hand contact with food. Provide serving utensils for employees and for customers who serve themselves.

- Use utensils, such as clean tongs, scoops, forks, spoons, spatulas, and similar items, with the proper foods. Each utensil should be used for only one food item.

- Use long-handled utensils that keep the server's hands away from food. Cups, bowls, and utensils with short handles should NOT be used for serving. The handles could easily contact the food.

- Use a spoon or another utensil to remove any serving or mixing spoon that falls into food. Do not put your fingers into food.

- While serving foods, keep utensils in the serving dish with the handle extending out of the food. Do not leave utensils exposed at room temperature (the danger zone). This can cause bacteria to grow on the utensil.

Customer Self-Service

Self-service operations such as cafeterias, salad bars, smorgasbords, and buffets are popular. Foods in these establishments are handled by many people, making it difficult to maintain proper holding and serving conditions. Foods always should be served in a way that minimizes contamination.

- Keep foods wrapped or covered when possible. Condiments are more hygienic when served in individual packages.

- Reduce contamination to exposed foods by placing an easy-to-clean, properly constructed "sneeze guard" (food guard) between the customer and the foods.

- Position serving dishes in such a way that it eliminates handling by customers.

- Provide enough serving utensils for each food presented. To avoid cross-contamination, each utensil should be used for only one food item.

- Store utensils so that food contact surfaces are not touched by customers. Also make sure that surfaces touched by hands do not contact food. Utensils should be exchanged frequently for clean, sanitized ones.

- Monitor temperatures of foods: Keep cold foods cold, keep hot foods hot. Foods must be kept out of the **danger zone**.

- Assign employees to monitor and maintain the cleanliness of the buffet.

Self-service customers who return to the service area for additional food should not reuse soiled tableware or utensils. Provide them with clean dishes. Cups and glasses for drinks may be refilled. Sugar, condiments, seasonings, or dressings used in self-service should be in individual packages or covered dispensers that protect their contents.

Transporting Food

Food and drink that are prepared at a food establishment but served at some other place must be stored, transported, displayed, and handled in a safe and sanitary manner at all times. When food is transported, the risk of contamination is great.

- Carry all food, serving equipment, and utensils in tightly covered containers or securely wrapped packages to protect them from contamination.

- Provide a supply of potable water at the remote site.

- Keep all foods, whether chilled or cooked, at constant, controlled temperatures at all times.

- Use insulated food carriers during transport or brief holding periods. Make sure that correct temperatures are maintained.

- Pre-chill foods that are to be served cold before you transport them. Keep them at a temperature of 41°F or below for storage and for service.

- Hold all foods that are to be served hot at a temperature of 140°F or above.

- Clean and sanitize units used to transport food between uses.

Temporary Food Service

Food setups used for sporting events, fairs, etc. which are only intended to provide temporary service must meet the same basic sanitation and safety criteria that permanent establishments maintain. Food is prepared at the permanent site and transported to the temporary unit.

- Cold foods and drinks must be kept at 41°F or below.

- Hot foods must be kept at 140°F or above.

- Potable water must be available in the temporary service.

Using Leftovers

Foods that have been exposed to sources of contamination should never be used again. Individual unwrapped portions of food that have been served to customers may not be used again.

You may use some cooked foods that were not served to customers if they were prepared safely and held under sanitary conditions. They must be cooled to 41°F for storage. Individually wrapped items with undamaged packaging may be reused.

If food is not to be used by your establishment but is safe to eat, check with local food pantries or soup kitchens before discarding. More than 20% of usable food in the United States is thrown out, and food establishments can help the hungry through donations to food charities.

It is not always possible to identify food spoilage by appearance, smell, or taste. Food may appear to be safe even though it may contain large numbers of harmful microorganisms or toxins. It is necessary to observe good food protection and sanitation practices in all phases of preparing and serving food. The main point to remember in choosing to serve previously prepared food is: **IF IN DOUBT, THROW IT OUT**.

Cooling Food

When cooked foods are to be refrigerated and stored for future use, they must be chilled as *quickly* as possible to an internal temperature of 41°F. If they are left at room temperature to cool, bacterial growth is likely.

- Divide large quantities of food into smaller or shallow portions.

- Place foods in shallow containers, of 2 inches deep or less, and stir to speed the cooling process.

- Use refrigerator units that are specially designed to chill food quickly.

Cool cooked and leftover foods rapidly.

- Use an ice-water bath: place pans of food into larger containers filled with ice to prc-cool if special refrigerator units are not available. Add ice periodically and stir the food in the pan to make sure that the entire contents chills rapidly.

- According to the 1995 FDA Food Code, cooked potentially hazardous foods must be cooled from 140°F to 70°F within 2 hours, and from 70°F to 41°F, or below, within 4 hours.

- If the prepared food was made from ingredients kept at room temperature, the food must be cooled to 41°F within 4 hours.

- Move quick-chilled foods to normal refrigeration within 3 to 4 hours.

- Do not try to cool too much cooked food at one time; it will strain the capacity of a refrigerator. You could endanger other foods by raising temperatures in the refrigerator.

Storing Leftover Food

Select storage containers carefully, especially for highly acidic foods, to avoid the dangers of chemical contamination.

- Pack all leftovers in labeled, well-covered, well-sealed containers. Shallow containers are recommended for storage because they cool faster.

- Store cooked and processed foods above and away from raw foods, to minimize the dangers of cross-contamination.

- Never store cooked foods below raw foods. Raw foods could drip contaminants into the stored foods. Some stored foods do not require reheating.

- Cool hot food as described above, then cover.

- Label containers clearly to indicate what they contain and when the food was prepared. Use FIFO for storage placement.

Store raw meat, poultry, fish, or eggs so they do not drip on cooked foods.

Reheating Food

When reheating leftovers, bring them within 2 hours to a temperature of 165°F throughout in the shortest amount of time or for 15 seconds. If using a microwave oven, food must be reheated to 190°F and allowed to stand covered for 2 minutes after reheating.

Use food preparation equipment to reheat leftovers. Do not use steam tables, heat lamps, or other food holding equipment to heat food. They are not designed for this use.

Summary

Food can easily become contaminated during the various stages of preparation and serving. Time and correct temperatures need to be monitored closely. Every food handler must know the correct procedures of food preparation and service. Furthermore, each employee needs to be trained to clean and sanitize equipment and utensils as often as needed and be motivated to practice good personal hygiene to guarantee safe food to your clients.

Chapter 5 Review Questions

1.   What temperature range is known as the *danger zone*?

2.   What are three proper ways to thaw food?

      A.

      B.

      C.

3.   How do you check the temperature of a beef roast?

4.   What are the minimum cooking temperatures for:

      A. Poultry and stuffed meats?

      B. Pork?

      C. Beef?

5.   Name at least two ways to cool foods properly:

      A.

      B.

6.   Foods must be reheated to an internal temperature of _____°F and held for serving at _____°F.

See Appendix E for answers.

CHAPTER 6
Equipment and Utensils

☞ *Food preparation requires the use of specialized equipment and utensils for cooking and serving. Proper selection, use, and care of these tools are the responsibility of the food service manager. Even if you are not responsible for choosing the original equipment, you must monitor maintenance and repairs. Knowing what is acceptable is your responsibility.*

Choosing Equipment and Utensils

The choice of equipment for cooking, serving, and cleaning will depend on many factors, such as the menu, the amount of food to be prepared, the number of people working in the area, the amount of workspace, and the budget.

Materials

Equipment and utensils should be constructed and repaired with safe materials that are corrosion resistant, not absorbent, smooth, easily cleanable, and durable under normal use. Equipment should carry the National Sanitation Foundation (NSF) or similar certification.

- Single-service articles must be made from clean, sanitary, safe materials and are not to be reused.

- All materials for equipment and utensils used in food establishments must not transmit any odor, color, or taste that could contaminate food.

- Wooden materials for cutting blocks, cutting boards, salad bowls, and baker's tables must be made of hard maple or equivalent nonabsorbent substance.

- Plastic and rubber or rubberlike equipment and utensils must be made of materials that are resistant (under normal use) to scratching, scoring, decomposition, chipping, and distortion. The equipment or utensil must be thick and heavy enough to withstand cleaning and sanitizing by normal dishwashing methods for repeated use.

Design and Fabrication

All equipment and utensils should be designed and fabricated for durability under normal use. These items must be resistant to denting, buckling, pitting, and chipping.

- Food contact surfaces must be easy to clean, smooth, free of breaks and imperfections, and promote easy cleaning of internal corners and crevices.

- Cast iron may be used as a food contact surface only if it is a cooking surface, as is the case with grills, griddle tops, and skillets.

- Tubing that carries beverages or beverage ingredients to dispensing heads may not come into contact or touch stored ice. This does not apply to cold plates that are constructed integrally with an ice storage bin. Drainage tubes from the dispenser must not pass through the ice or storage bin. They must be installed directly to a floor or hub drain or other connection to the sewer.

- Equipment containing bearings and gears requiring lubricants that are not safe for food must be designed so that the lubricant cannot leak, drip, or be forced into or onto food contact surfaces. Approved lubricants may be used on equipment designed to receive lubrication of bearings and gears that may contact food surfaces.

- Sinks and drainboards must be self-draining.

Accessibility

If equipment is not designed to be taken apart, all food contact surfaces must be easy to reach for cleaning and inspection. Equipment that is to be taken apart without tools or taken apart easily with simple tools such as a screwdriver or an opened wrench kept near the equipment must be easy to clean and inspect.

In-Place Cleaning

Equipment designed for nonmobile or stationary cleaning must be designed and fabricated so that:

- Cleaning and sanitizing solutions can be circulated throughout fixed systems using an effective cleaning and sanitizing procedure

- Cleaning and sanitizing solutions come into contact with all interior surfaces

- The system is self-draining or capable of being completely drained of the cleaning and sanitizing solutions.

Pressure Spray Cleaning

Wiring, electrical switches, and connections have to be sealed completely if pressure spray cleaning is used.

Thermometers

Thermometers used for immersion into food or cooking media (oil, water, etc.) must be metal stemmed, numerically scaled, and accurate to plus or minus 2°F.

Non-Food Contact Surfaces

Surfaces of equipment not intended for contact with food but which receive splashes of food, debris, or require frequent cleaning must be fabricated and designed to be smooth, washable, free of unnecessary projections or cracks, and easy to clean.

Ventilation Hoods

Ventilation hoods and devices are used to prevent grease or moisture condensation from collecting on walls, ceilings, equipment, or dripping onto food.

Filters or other grease extractors must be easy to remove, clean, or replace.

Equipment Installation and Location

Do not locate equipment, including ice makers and ice storage equipment, under exposed pipes, unprotected sewer or water lines, open stairwells, or other sources of contamination. Fire sprinkler heads, required by law, are exempt from this rule.

Table-Mounted Equipment

Equipment placed on tables or counters, unless portable, must be sealed to the table or counter, or elevated on legs at least 4 inches to allow easy cleaning of the equipment and surrounding areas. The food contact surfaces of cooking equipment must be cleaned at least every 24 hours. More frequent cleaning is needed for equipment that comes in contact with raw foods or potentially hazardous foods. Consult your local health department for required cleaning and sanitizing.

Portable equipment is defined as equipment that can be moved easily by one person; has a utility connection that disconnects quickly, or has a flexible utility connection line long enough to allow the equipment to be moved easily for cleaning.

Floor-Mounted Equipment

Floor-mounted equipment, unless easily movable, must be:

*   Sealed to the floor

*   Installed on a raised platform of masonry or concrete that is sealed to the floor or elevated for clearance

*   Elevated or have legs that provide at least 6 inches of clearance between the floor and equipment.

Vertically mounted floor mixers may be elevated to provide at least a 4-inch clearance between the floor and equipment, provided that no part of the floor under the mixer is more than 6 inches from cleaning access.

Movable Equipment

Equipment is easily movable if:

*   It is mounted on wheels or casters and has a utility connection that disconnects quickly, or has a flexible utility line long enough to be moved easily for cleaning

*   The space between, behind, and beside each unit of the floor-mounted equipment must be easy to reach for cleaning. (If the equipment is exposed to seepage, it must be sealed to the adjoining equipment or adjoining walls.)

Aisles and Working Spaces

The aisles and working spaces between the equipment must be wide enough to allow employees room to work without contaminating the food or food contact surfaces with clothing or by personal contact.

Carts, storage equipment, racks, and dollies that can be moved easily must be positioned so that access to the work areas is clear.

Large Equipment

Placement

Equipment should be placed to establish the most efficient flow of work. A correctly designed layout increases productivity. A well-organized flow of traffic in the kitchen and other work areas will promote quick, easy, and safe food handling practices. Analyze the work flow even if the facility is already set up. Are clean areas kept separate from contaminated workstations? Could any change be made to help guarantee food safety?

- Locate food storage areas (refrigerators and freezers) near the receiving area to avoid delays in storing perishable foods.

- Place refrigerators near preparation areas so that chilled foods are not removed until the moment they are needed and so that it is easy to store foods rapidly upon completion of preparation.

- Arrange equipment so that it can be cleaned easily and thoroughly. Do not leave spaces and cracks under, behind, or beside equipment where insects and microorganisms can hide.

- Keep food preparation equipment out of walkways.

- Locate equipment away from areas where garbage and other wastes are handled.

- Do not store dirty dishes or linens in or near food preparation equipment.

Refrigerators and Freezers

Design

- Commercial refrigerators and freezers should be constructed of durable materials that do not rust, with doors that seal well and easy-to-clean surfaces.

- Interiors should not have places where dirt and food particles can collect.

- Interiors should have sufficient light with bulbs protected against breakage.

- Shelves should be open-slatted and easy to remove for cleaning.

- Condensation from the coils of a refrigeration unit must not collect and drip onto food.

- Drains, except those for condensation, should not be located inside the cabinet of the unit. Condensation drains must be kept clean and working.

Two types of refrigerators are commonly used in food service establishments, walk-in and reach-in.

- Reach-in refrigerators should be mounted on a base or raised 6 inches off the floor for easy cleaning. Units equipped with casters that make movement easy for cleaning also are acceptable.

- Walk-in refrigerators must be sealed to the floor and wall with vinyl mopboard or silicone caulking.

- A walk-in refrigerator must have a handle on the inside so that employees will not be trapped inside.

Temperature

Refrigerator temperatures should range between 38 and 40°F. Check local regulations for your area. Refrigerators must:

- Be monitored frequently for temperature control with easy-to-read air-space thermometers

- Be checked regularly to make sure that thermometers are accurate to plus or minus 3°F; and if a thermometer cannot be calibrated, it must be replaced

- Be monitored in several areas of the unit, especially in the warmest part since temperatures vary within each refrigeration unit

- Be checked to see if internal temperatures of refrigerated foods, as well as air temperature, have reached recommended levels

- Have food temperatures checked at the end of each shift with a metal stemmed thermometer

- Have foods stored in the correct part of the refrigerator (for example, meat in the coldest area)

Proper Use

Refrigerators and freezers will protect food efficiently if they are used correctly. Be sure that all employees are trained and that they always follow proper procedures.

- Do not overload. Overloading can cause the air temperature in the unit to rise into the danger zone.

- Do not use storage refrigerators to quick-chill hot items. Raising temperatures will overwork the equipment and possibly endanger stored food.

- Do not use refrigeration units for general dry storage.

- Wrap completely cooled food securely or store in covered containers.

- Label and date foods. Use them as soon as possible. Use the FIFO rule.

- Check coolers and freezers daily for spoiled foods. Check codes and dates. Throw out any food that is in question.

- Keep doors closed as much as possible.

Maintenance

Always keep refrigeration units clean and sanitized, inside and out.

- Wash all walls, floors, and shelves, and especially gaskets, on a routine basis.

- Clean baked-enamel or stainless steel surfaces with a mild soap or detergent solution. Rinse with clear water or a baking soda solution.

- Defrost coolers and freezers before cleaning unless they defrost automatically.

- Defrost freezers when frost is thicker than 1/4 inch; frost reduces airflow, which makes the freezer function poorly.

- Inspect doors for leaky or torn gaskets and broken hinges or latches.

- Keep condensation drains clean and working to avoid odor, rusting, and unsanitary conditions.

- Keep fan guards free of rust, dust, and mold.

Refrigeration units should receive regular maintenance by employees and by a trained specialist and have routine maintenance to keep the evaporator and condenser fins, coils, etc. clean and clear of rust, dust, and mold. This will also improve the efficiency of the unit, allow easier temperature maintenance, use less electricity, and cause less wear and tear on the compressor. These are all bottom-line money-saving ideas.

Dishwashing Machines

Dishwashing machines must be carefully operated and maintained.

Requirements and Maintenance

Each machine has its own operating procedures, which must be followed carefully. The manufacturer's instructions should be affixed to the machine and specify proper temperatures, speeds, running times, and amount of detergent. General instructions are listed in Chapter 7.

Operating instructions, including the right water pressure, should be posted in an easy-to-see place on the machine. All employees who operate dishwashing equipment should be carefully trained. Following proper procedures and monitoring the equipment will mean fewer breakdowns, but more important, the dishes and utensils will be properly cleaned and sanitized.

- Purchase commercial equipment designed to handle the needs of the establishment.

- Never overload dishwashers.

- Use the thermometers mounted in the machine to indicate the water temperature of each tank of the machine and the temperature of the final rinse water.

- Check thermometers and timers often to be sure they are correct.

- Check the gauge cock to measure water pressure upstream of the final rinse valve. Maintain line pressure between 15 and 25 pounds per square inch.

- Remove curtains, trays, and spray arms and clean dishwashers before use and, if used, at least every 24 hours.

- Use only potable water in dishwashing equipment.

- Keep mineral deposits from building up, especially in areas where hard water is used. Follow instructions on acid cleaners intended to remove deposits.

- Sinks and drainboards must be self-draining.

Utensils for Preparing and Serving Food

Use and Storage

The utensils you use for preparing and serving food must meet standards of safety and sanitation. They must be handled and stored in ways that protect them from damage and contamination.

- Never use utensils and equipment made of toxic metals that could contaminate food.

- Select long-handled utensils that keep servers' hands away from food.

- Do not use cups, bowls, or utensils with short handles for serving food.

- Provide separate, well-protected areas for washing and storing all utensils and small equipment, as well as for tableware, silverware, and linens.

- Do not store glassware or dishes on towels or materials that remain wet.

- Do not line utensil storage drawers with paper or plastic materials; dust, food particles, and roaches can find their way under the lining.

Summary

A good food service establishment will select and use the kind of equipment and utensils that facilitate the production of safe food. Cleaning, sanitizing, and maintaining the equipment should be done regularly. People need to be well-trained to perform these duties.

Chapter 6 Review Questions

1. Table-mounted equipment should be sealed to the table or counter, or be elevated on legs that are at least _____ inches tall.

2. What are some considerations for placement of large equipment?

    A.

    B.

    C.

    D.

3. How much clearance should floor-mounted equipment leave for cleaning?

4. Where in the refrigerator should thermometers be located?

See Appendix E for answers.

CHAPTER 7
Cleaning, Sanitizing, and Pest Control

 Proper cleaning and sanitizing help protect all who eat or work in a food service establishment. A safe environment is maintained by keeping utensils, equipment, and work areas free of dirt, contamination, and pests.

The Importance of Cleaning and Sanitizing

Safe food service is only possible with a clean and sanitary environment in which to store, process, and serve foods. Keeping equipment, utensils, and work areas cleaned and sanitized is an important part of preparing safe food. Proper housekeeping practices reduce the risks of both chemical and physical contamination. Cleaning and sanitizing procedures reduce the risks of biological contamination.

Cleaning alone is not enough to maintain a healthy food service establishment. Even when dirt and food particles have been removed from food contact surfaces, they are not ready to use. You must sanitize to kill the bacteria that could contaminate foods you prepare and serve. Washing with detergent and hot water helps destroy some bacteria, but sanitizing with heat or chemical agents after cleaning does much more.

You can reduce bacteria to safe levels using proper cleaning and sanitizing techniques.

Equipment and food surfaces come into contact with bacteria and dirt all day long. **Wash, rinse, and sanitize** equipment and surfaces thoroughly and often, usually every time they are used. Organize your workspace to make the task easier. A knowledge of correct procedures will help a food service manager keep the equipment clean and sanitary.

Contamination is spread by kitchen equipment not properly cleaned.

Cleaning and Sanitizing Procedures

Manual Cleaning and Sanitizing

Equipment and utensils that cannot be cleaned in automatic dishwashers may be cleaned and sanitized by hand. Large sinks with at least three compartments and attached drainboards are recommended. Each compartment should have hot and cold potable water. You must clean the sinks after each use.

Washing, rinsing, sanitizing, and air-drying must be done in separate steps. Drainboards or movable dish tables should be used to separate dirty utensils from clean utensils before washing.

Properly wash, rinse, and sanitize all kitchen equipment and utensils.

- Scrape or soak equipment and utensils to remove large food particles and dirt.

- The temperature of the wash solution should be maintained at not less than 110°F unless a different temperature is specified on the cleaning agent manufacturer's label instructions.

- Rinse utensils in clean, hot water until they are free of all detergents and abrasives.

- To sanitize utensils, immerse them in an approved chemical and water solution at a temperature of at least 75°F for 1 minute or more. Follow the product instructions to get the correct amount and strength, equivalent to 50 ppm (parts per million) of chlorine, 12.5 ppm of iodine, or 200 ppm of quaternary ammonium. Use a test kit to monitor the proper strength of solutions. Sanitizing solutions should not be used after the strength goes below minimum requirements.

-OR-

- You could use a dish basket to immerse (dip) the utensils in clean, very hot water (170°F) or above for 30 seconds.

- Equipment too large for the sink compartment should first be washed and rinsed, then sprayed or wiped by hand, using chlorine, iodine, or quaternary ammonium solutions.

- Follow the sanitizing process, air-dry utensils and tableware; never dry them with a towel.

- Use cleaned and sanitized drainboards or movable dish tables to stack and transport sanitized utensils.

Mechanical Cleaning and Sanitizing

Machines are generally better than manual washing for cleaning and sanitizing utensils and equipment. Machines can easily handle large amounts of items and high water temperatures. They can regulate temperatures automatically and spray water at and over dirty tableware, utensils, and equipment. Machines also distribute cleaning and sanitizing agents evenly during the process in the right strengths.

Operating Dishwashing and Sanitizing Machines

Procedures vary a lot from model to model, and the manufacturer's operating and maintenance instructions must be followed carefully to get the best results. Certain basic rules are the same for operating all types of machines.

Dishwashing machines are made to handle a large volume of items at one time. Organize your workspace so that dirty dishes and equipment are held safely until they can be washed. Do not let them contact and contaminate food that is being prepared or equipment that has already been cleaned. Use drainboards or movable dish tables for this purpose.

- Always scrape dishes by hand before loading the machine. Pre-soaking or scrubbing may also be necessary to remove stubborn food particles.

- When loading the machine, place dishes and utensils in the racks, trays, or baskets. In this way the rinse water reaches all dirty surfaces and can drain properly.

- Always use the right amounts of detergent and chemicals for washing and sanitizing. Load the machine according to operating instructions.

- In a mechanical operation, the temperature of the fresh hot water sanitizing rinse as it enters the manifold should not be less than 180°F except for a single-tank stationary-rack single-temperature machine, which should be 165°F.

- After sanitization, all equipment and utensils must be air dried.

Regulating Water Temperature and Pressure

Water temperature and pressure of the machines should be set correctly and checked often. Always operate the equipment at the manufacturer's recommendations. Check to make sure that the following conditions are met:

- Wash water should generally be between 150 and 165°F.

- The minimum final rinse water temperature for a single-tank stationary-rack single-temperature machine is 165°F. For all other machines it should be 180°F.

- Machine or waterline-mounted thermometers, accurate to within 3°F, must indicate the temperature of the water in each tank of the machine and the temperature of the final rinse water as it enters the manifold. There are also one-time-use, maximum-temperature-indicating thermometers available that stick to dishes.

- Rinse water tanks should be separated by baffles, curtains, or other ways to separate wash water from rinse water.

- Timers on all machines, especially those that regulate conveyor belts, should be accurate. Check timers to be sure that wash loads are given the proper exposure times in wash and rinse cycles.

Machines can be of the single-tank, stationary-rack, door-type, and spray-type glass washer varieties that use chemicals for sanitization, provided that:

- The temperature of the wash water is not less than 120°F.

- Chemicals added for sanitization purposes are automatically dispensed in the proper strength.

- Approved chemical sanitizers are used.

- Utensils and equipment go through the final chemical sanitizing rinse for the proper time.

- The chemical sanitizing rinse water temperature is not less than 75°F nor less than the temperature specified by the machine's manufacturer. Rinse water temperature should not be above 120°F in chemical sanitizing machines.

- A test kit or other device that accurately measures the parts per million concentration of the solution is used.

Storage of Equipment and Tableware

- Store clean sanitized utensils and equipment at least 6 inches above the floor in a clean, dry location. In this way they are protected from contamination by splash, dust, and other sources.

- Always air-dry utensils before putting them away. Store them upside down in a self-draining position.

- Store items so that you can pick them up without touching the food contact surfaces. Glasses and cups should be stored upside down. Knives, forks, and spoons should be arranged so that they can be picked up by the handles.

- Protect the food contact surfaces of stationary equipment from contamination.

- Do not store food equipment, utensils, or single-service articles in rest rooms or other areas with possible contaminants.

- Do not store food equipment, utensils, or single-service articles on towels. Store only on nonabsorbent, easily cleanable surfaces.

Stationary Equipment

Disassemble stationary food preparation equipment and clean and sanitize it according to the manufacturer's instructions. These are the best procedures, and using them is the surest way to protect your warranty rights. The cleaning methods for almost any large or electrically powered equipment will include the following:

- Disconnect the power.

- Disassemble the equipment to wash, rinse, and sanitize the individual parts. Immerse them in a sink if possible.

- Wash and rinse all remaining surfaces.

- Sanitize all food contact surfaces with chemical sanitizing solution.

- Wipe down all other surfaces with sanitizing solution.

- Let all parts air-dry before putting the equipment back together.

- Resanitize any food contact surface that was touched when the equipment was reassembled.

Stationary equipment and utensils and equipment too large to be cleaned in a sink should be washed by hand or cleaned through pressure spray methods. Rinse, spray, or swab equipment with sanitizing solution.

If suggested by the manufacturer, you may clean the interior of some equipment which pumps or circulates liquids by circulating cleaning and sanitizing solutions. **Do not allow chemical solutions and rinses to flow into other parts of the machine.** It is always best to follow the manufacturer's instructions.

Some equipment can also be cleaned and sanitized with the use of power spray equipment. Spray the object for 2 or 3 minutes with the sanitizing solution. You may also use live steam if it is clean.

The food contact surfaces of stationary equipment must be covered or otherwise protected when not in use.

Cleaning Products

Detergent compounds are usually added to aid the removal of soil. They make the process of cleaning easier and faster by reducing the physical effort of scrubbing and by attacking stubborn types of soil. Detergents are designed to loosen grease and oil, deposits of minerals, protein-based stains caused by eggs or meat, and dirt that has been baked onto food contact surfaces. The amount of detergent to use per quantity of water must be measured carefully according to the manufacturer's instructions. The detergent aids in loosening the food particles, but you still have to brush the surfaces either by machine or by hand.

After scrubbing and washing, everything has to be thoroughly rinsed. The surfaces must be clean before sanitizing. Any residue of detergent left on surfaces can interfere with proper sanitizing.

Use the right cleaning agent for each job and use the product correctly. Choose a product that will do the job thoroughly, economically, and safely in the recommended concentrations.

There are three main groups of cleaning products used for loosening and removing dirt:

- Detergents

- Acid cleaners

- Abrasive cleaners

Detergents

Synthetic detergents are used with water to break down dirt. All detergents contain agents called *surfactants* that dissolve in water and spread by means of suds. They work by loosening the dirt, making it easier to remove. Detergents are usually not very expensive. They are also among the most effective all-purpose cleaning products.

Detergents, if rinsed properly, do not leave a soapy residue and make it easier to clean a surface. They also work well with chemical sanitizers. Detergents can be used to clean food contact surfaces.

Acid Cleaners

Acid cleaners work by loosening the heavier dirt that alkaline-based detergents cannot remove. The product labels will say which jobs and surfaces these acid cleaners are designed for and what strength the concentration should be. **Follow the instructions for these products carefully.** Acid cleaning agents, even when used in low concentrations, may damage surfaces and cause chemical burns on the employee's skin.

Abrasive Cleansers

Be cautious when using abrasive cleansers. The scrubbing power is provided by finely ground minerals that scour the surface to remove encrusted soil. Food contact surfaces made of soft plastics can scratch easily and become less resistant to bacteria. When abrasive cleansers are used, care must be taken to rinse away all of the scouring agent after the scrubbing.

Sanitizing Products

Sanitizing is a most important step in protecting the food service establishment. Equipment, utensils, and surfaces are sanitized, after cleaning and rinsing, to kill bacteria that may still be present on food contact surfaces. Equipment and surfaces may be sanitized either by using hot water or chemical compounds.

Hot-Water Sanitizing

When using hot water as a sanitizer, the water must stay at a temperature of at least 170°F, which will probably require a booster heater. The water temperature must be checked often. To prevent burns, a dish basket must be used for dipping. All equipment and utensils should be completely held under the water for at least 30 seconds to sanitize.

Chemical Sanitizing

Sanitizers are chemicals designed to destroy microorganisms. Chemical sanitizers are more frequently used then hot water for sanitizing. Sanitizing solutions contain bacteria-killing chemicals and are used after the equipment has been cleaned and rinsed.

Approved chemical sanitizers include chlorine, iodine, and quaternary ammonium. Read the directions and follow all instructions provided by the manufacturer.

Chlorine Compounds

Chlorine compounds usually work well in soft or hard water. They are relatively non-irritating when used in the proper concentrations, but they can cause damage to metal equipment. Thorough rinsing before using chlorine compounds is important because their effectiveness is reduced by alkalines left behind by detergents. Water temperature should be 75°F.

Iodine Compounds

Iodine compounds work well in hard water, do not irritate the user's skin, and are useful for metal or rubber surfaces because they are less corrosive than chlorine. Iodine has an amber color. The stronger the concentration, the darker the color. Some facilities prefer using iodine for this reason. Water temperature should be between 75 and 120°F.

Quaternary Ammonium Compounds

These compounds, also called **quats**, are usually safe for skin contact and generally do not damage equipment. Some do not work well when used with very hard water or after using certain detergents, but they usually work well in both acid and alkaline solutions. Water temperature should be 75°F.

Combination detergent-sanitizers, which contain both types of agents, are available. If these products are used to treat food service equipment, they must be used twice (once to clean and a second time to sanitize), with the proper concentrations, times, and temperatures for both tasks.

Concentration of Sanitizers

Product directions state the amount of sanitizer to add to water. You must have a test kit to measure the strength of sanitizing solutions during use. Chemical sanitizing can be done by complete immersion (dipping) of utensils and equipment for at least 1 minute in a clean sanitizing solution. A sanitizing solution must contain one of the following:

*   A minimum of 50 parts per million (ppm) of chlorine mixed with water

*   A minimum of 12.5 ppm of iodine mixed with water with a pH value below 5.0

*   A minimum of 200 ppm of quaternary ammonium compounds mixed with water

The minimum temperature of a chlorine solution is based on the concentration and pH of the solution.

Minimum Concentration	Minimum Temperature (°F)	
(mg/L)	pH 10 or less	pH 8 or less
25	120	120
50	100	75
100	55	55

It is important to keep the water at the required temperature when using chemical sanitizers. If the temperature is too high, the chemical is not effective. Check the strength of the sanitizer with test strips and monitor temperatures. Do not go over the maximum recommended strengths for sanitizers. Increasing the strength does not make the product work better. Quaternary ammonium compounds are not recommended at levels above 200 ppm. You waste money and risk leaving an unpleasant taste or odor, or even a toxic residue, if the solution is too strong. Follow the manufacturer's instructions on how to mix proper concentrations. **Do not rinse after sanitizing**. Sanitizing is the final step of the wash–rinse–sanitize cycle.

Wiping Supplies

Cloths and sponges used for wiping certain equipment, utensils, and food contact surfaces should not be used for any other purposes. These cloths should be kept separate from other wiping cloths.

*   Use only clean, dry cloths for wiping food spills on tableware, such as plates or bowls being served to the customer. These cloths must be used for no other purpose.

- Wipe food spills on kitchenware and food contact surfaces of equipment with moist cloths. They must be rinsed frequently in a sanitizing solution during use. These cloths must be used for no other purpose and should be stored in the sanitizing solution between uses.

Cleaning cloths and sponges can spread contamination.

- Wash and rinse cloths that are used on non-food contact surfaces of equipment, such as counters and dining tabletops, then rinse them in a sanitizing solution. These cloths must be used for no other purpose and are stored in the sanitizing solution between uses.

- Discard cloths as soon as they show signs of wear.

- If disposable towels are used in place of wiping cloths or sponges, the towels should be thrown out at least on a daily basis.

Frequency of Cleaning and Sanitizing

All equipment, utensils, and preparation surfaces should be cleaned and sanitized after **each use.** Microorganisms can survive on unclean tableware and utensils as well as in food. Washing, rinsing, and sanitizing utensils after use is the first step. Equipment must be protected from contamination when in storage and in use.

General

- Establish and follow regular, evenly spaced cleaning schedules.

- Teach employees why, how, and when cleaning will take place. Tell them what their responsibilities are. Create a cleaning schedule.

- Do not allow dirt and food particles to accumulate on any part or surface of standing equipment.

- Clean and sanitize warm work areas, where bacteria grow faster, as soon as you notice spills or splash.

After Each Use

- Clean and sanitize utensils after every use.

- Clean and sanitize all large stationary equipment and surfaces that come into contact with food after each use.

- Clean and sanitize utensils, equipment, and food preparation surfaces after contact with each potentially hazardous food item. This includes raw meat, dairy products, poultry, and eggs.

- Clean and sanitize food contact surfaces between use with raw and prepared products.

- Clean and sanitize all food contact surfaces regularly. When you wipe areas clean, sanitize them manually.

Several Times a Day

- Clean and sanitize equipment that is used all day long at periodic intervals during the workday when using for the same product. If the product is changed, sanitize after each change.

- Clean most cooking equipment several times a day to remove grease and food particles. Especially remove food matter from grills and other food contact surfaces.

- Clean the areas around ovens or hot oil cookers several times a day even when in use.

Once a Day

- Clean knobs, handles, oven doors, and areas around burners at least once a day.

- Food contact surfaces of grills, griddles, and microwave ovens must be cleaned at least once a day.

Maintaining Sanitary Facilities

Cleaning Procedures

Floors and Walls

You must have and be able to maintain a clean and orderly food service establishment for sanitary food preparation and service. Cleaning prevents the contamination of food and equipment, discourages the presence of insects and rodents, and keeps work and dining areas safe.

Facilities must be designed for cleanability and cleaned regularly. Set up cleaning schedules for all parts of your food service establishment and make sure that everyone knows when to clean and how to do it.

Facilities must be cleaned in the right way. Cleaning methods such as sweeping or pressure spraying may raise dust, scatter debris, or create mists that could contaminate food. Your responsibility as a manager includes knowing the correct method for cleaning.

Floors, mats, walls, ceilings, attached equipment, and decorative materials all need regular cleaning.

- Clean floors and walls when the least amount of food is out in the open, such as after closing or between mealtimes.

- Use only dustless methods of cleaning floors and walls, such as vacuum cleaning, wet cleaning, or sweeping compounds used with push brooms.

- Use detergent, scrubbing, and rinsing to remove dirt and grease.

- Post warning signs if floors must be wet during operation of the food service.

- Wipe up spills immediately to avoid contamination and accidents.

Cleaning Equipment

Maintain and store cleaning tools such as brooms, mops, vacuum cleaners, and similar equipment in a way that does not contaminate food, utensils, equipment, or linens. Keep them neatly stored in an easy-to-reach area.

- Provide a storage area for cleaning equipment and supplies that is located away from food preparation, storage, and serving areas.

- Launder cleaning equipment such as mops and washcloths regularly, but separately from linens.

- Store mops with mopheads off the floor for proper air drying.

- Reserve one utility sink or curbed cleaning facility with a floor drain which is used only for cleaning mops and similar tools. This sink is used for throwing away mop water and liquid wastes. Do not use sinks where dishes, utensils, or equipment is cleaned and sanitized. Do not pour mop water on the ground. Mop water is sewage and must be handled in the same way as sewage waste.

Pest Control

Animals and pests can cause illnesses to people by contaminating food and food contact surfaces. The best way to keep pests out is by making sure they cannot get in. Make sure that walls and floors have no holes. Doors must close automatically, open to the outside, and should have a tight fit. All windows, doors, skylights, intake and exhaust air ducts, and other openings to the outside must have screens. The mesh of screens should be at least small enough to prevent entry of pests, and they should not have holes or tears in them.

Store food supplies properly, clean and sanitize regularly, and dispose of trash frequently. This will reduce the food supply for pests.

Even with good sanitation and housekeeping, rodents and insects may be present in a food establishment. Insects may come from deliveries of packaged goods or from improperly stored trash outside the establishment. You need to know how to prevent pests from coming into areas where food is stored, prepared, and served, and where garbage is stored. You must also know about methods of killing any pests that do get in.

Pests

The best way to prevent pest infestation is to keep pests out of the establishment. However, since insects and pests have many ways of getting into food establishments, the best approach to insect and pest control is to hire a professional. A reliable, licensed PCO (pest control operator) will work with you to develop an ongoing pest control program, which should include **prevention**, **repairs**, **chemicals**, **traps**, etc.

Roaches

Roaches contaminate food from the dirt and bacteria they carry. Roaches can be found in places where food and water are available. Signs of droppings and empty eggshells are indications of the presence of roaches. In the case of roaches it is especially important to keep the establishment clean and neat.

Ants

Ants may live outside or inside walls, traveling from their nests through cracks, electrical conduits, or plumbing. Ants may contaminate any food.

House Flies and Other Flying Insects

Flies land on all surfaces. They transmit bacteria by leaving dirt from their feet, their own excrement, and their own vomitus. Flies vomit on food to dissolve the solid and then suck up the liquid, leaving behind the bacteria from the vomitus. In this way they pass on many different kinds of diseases. Flies must be kept out of food areas. It is important to eliminate all breeding sites and to have good screens, self-closing doors, air curtains, or fans.

Other flying insects, such as bees, wasps, hornets, and yellow jackets, can also present hazards around a food establishment.

Pantry Pests

A variety of insects can enter an establishment by way of ingredients. Bran beetles may be found in packages of flour and dry mixes. Several other tiny beetles deposit small, light-colored eggs in grain products. Weevils hide in dried beans and peas. The rice weevil gets into whole grains, macaroni, noodles, and spaghetti. Hide and larder beetles like cheese, smoked and cured meats, and organic debris. They are sometimes found around incinerators. The cereal mite is often found in cereals and cereal products. It is hardly visible, but large numbers of the mites can leave a mass of gray powder from dropped skins. Their presence can mean that the product in which they are hiding has a higher-than-normal moisture content.

Store poisons in separate rooms from foods.

Rats and Mice

Rats are good climbers and can squeeze through small openings. Both rats and mice can gnaw through wood. Rats and mice will eat a variety of food. They like to take their food into hiding but eat large items in place. You can tell they are around by signs of gnawing and burrowing, droppings, tracks, and signs of grease and dirt that show the paths they take to their nests.

Birds

Birds can be pests to food service operations. Birds and their droppings can easily contaminate food, especially in the open air around the food establishment. Birds can also pass on dangerous diseases.

Controlling Insects

Electrocutor Devices ("Zappers")

Insect electrocutors can be used to control insects. These devices should be designed to have "escape-resistant" trays. Check local codes and rules to determine if there is any jurisdictional restriction. Use properly installed and maintained insect electrocutors in receiving areas, halls, and garbage areas. Do not locate over a food preparation area as dead insects could fall onto food, food preparation surfaces, or equipment and utensils. Hang the devices low and away from open food and equipment. Vapor lights may be used outdoors, but they should be placed away from entrances so they do not attract flying bugs to these areas. Clean the collection trays at least once a week, since they may attract pests that feed on dead bugs.

Traps

Devices used to trap insects by adherence may not be installed above exposed food; clean equipment, utensils, and linens; or unwrapped single-service and single-use articles.

Repellents

Repellents are used to keep insects away from an area, but they do not kill bugs. Repellents can be purchased in spray, powder, or liquid form and may be applied around the outside of walls or other areas that are difficult to reach. Use them carefully, because these chemicals may create health hazards when used near areas where food is stored, prepared, or served.

Sprays

Three different types of insecticide sprays are available for killing cockroaches and flies.

- Residual sprays are applied directly to surfaces in a thin layer. The deposit kills insects when they touch it.

- Contact sprays, which must touch the insect to kill it, are usually applied to a group of insects, such as a cluster of ants in a corner or crack.

- A space spray, or fogger, discharges a mist into the air for killing bugs. Since space sprays can easily contaminate food, they should be used only by a licensed pest control operator.

Before an area is sprayed, remove all foods and food contact utensils to avoid contamination. Sprays should not be used near exposed food, food preparation and serving areas, or food contact surfaces. Cover everything that cannot be moved and cleaned after spraying.

Only use insecticides approved for use in food service areas and follow the manufacturer's instructions carefully. Check local rules and regulations for specific information before using any insecticides or pesticides.

Killing Rats and Mice

If rodents come into your food service establishment, you must know how to kill them. One sure way to discourage them is by depriving them of food, water, and shelter.

Traps

For small numbers of rodents, traps may be enough. They offer a slow but safe method of killing rats and mice. Use fresh ground meat, pet food, cheese, bacon, or peanut butter as bait and replace the bait regularly to keep it fresh. Place the traps at right angles to rodent paths, with the baited or trigger end toward the wall, and check them daily. All bait must be contained in a covered bait station.

Glue Boards

Glue boards are especially suited for use in food service areas because they do not contain poisons. Place them where there are signs of rats or mice, check them daily, and remove them as soon as a rat or mouse is trapped. Be advised that glue boards are less effective than other methods of controlling rats. They are particularly effective for ants and roaches.

Poisons and Pesticides

Poisons and pesticides can be as deadly to people as to rodents. Use them only as a last resort in the killing of rats and mice, with the advice of a licensed pest control operator. Jobs such as **misting, dusting,** and **gassing** should be performed ONLY by a licensed exterminator.

The safest and most commonly used poisons are multiple-dose anticoagulants. They must be eaten several times by rodents to kill them. The lower concentrations provide a safety factor that protects humans who may eat the poison accidentally.

Prepare bait according to package directions. Place bait outside food areas along rodent runways and breeding sites, and write down where you put them. Inspect the baits daily and replace them when necessary. Be very careful when using poisons to kill rats and mice. Never place baits where they might be confused with food items or where they may contaminate food, food service areas, equipment, or utensils. Be sure that poisons cannot be reached and eaten accidentally by children and pets.

When pesticides are used in a food service establishment, several precautions must be taken.

- Store all pesticides properly, in their original containers. If transferred to another container, they must be clearly labeled.

- Follow the package directions carefully and use the least amount of poison that will do the job. Do not put out more than necessary.

- Recognize the different uses of oil and water-based sprays.

- Avoid any possibility of contaminating food or food contact surfaces.

- Store insecticides and rodenticides away from detergents, sanitizers, related cleaning or drying agents, caustics, acids, polishes, and other chemicals.

- Post in a highly visible location emergency treatment procedures in case of accidental poisoning.

Summary

Cleaning, sanitizing, and aggressive pest control contribute significantly to the ability to serve safe food. Protecting food from contamination is a total commitment that must be made to lower the number of foodborne illness outbreaks. The ultimate responsibility for pest control is yours. Your establishment must be regularly inspected and treated. After insect spraying and/or fumigating, all food contact items and surfaces must be cleaned and sanitized to protect people.

Chapter 7 Review Questions

1. What must be done to finish the cleaning process after utensils and equipment are washed and rinsed?

2. Put the following cleaning steps in the correct order:

    wash

    sanitize

    rinse

    air dry

    scrape

3. What should water temperatures be for:

    A. manual dish washing?

    B. machine dish washing?

    C. the final rinse in a dishwasher?

4. List two ways to do manual sanitizing. Describe the steps involved.

    A.

    B.

5. How do you accurately measure the strength of sanitizing solutions?

6. Where should wiping cloths used for counters be stored between uses?

7.   Why is it important to eliminate pests from the food service environment?

8.   Which of the following must be done by a licensed pest control operator?

    A.   gassing

    B.   dusting

    C.   spraying

    D.   fumigating

See Appendix E for answers.

CHAPTER 8
Facilities

☞ *For a food service establishment to be clean and safe, the facilities must be constructed with good ventilation and plumbing systems. These systems lower the chances of contamination in the food service area. Again, you may not be involved in the original construction, but maintenance and remodeling could be a part of your job.*

Design and Materials

A well-designed food service establishment is one that is easy to clean and maintain.

If you are building or remodeling, choose a floor plan that will give you separate, clean areas for the various food service operations. This will reduce traffic and the risk of contamination. Approval by health and construction authorities is required for your plans before you begin construction or remodeling.

Walls and Ceilings

Walls and ceilings must be properly built and kept in good repair. Surfaces should be sealed or covered with smooth, nonabsorbent materials so that they are easy to clean. Concrete or pumice blocks used for interior wall construction must be finished and sealed. Studs, joists, and rafters should not be exposed in food preparation areas, walk-ins, rest rooms, or dishwashing areas. If they are exposed in other areas, they should be painted to provide an easily cleanable surface and be kept clean. Temporary walls, doors, windows, skylights, and similar closures should also be easy to clean and maintain.

Walls and ceilings should be painted in a light color. This is especially true for walk-in refrigerators, food preparation areas, equipment and utensil washing areas, and rest rooms. Light colors help to distribute light that makes soil easier to see and permits thorough cleaning and sanitary food preparation.

Floors

Materials

Floors should be smooth and properly constructed of durable, nonabsorbent materials, such as sealed concrete, cement, terrazzo, or quarry tile. Other acceptable floor covering materials include ceramic tile, durable grades of linoleum or plastic, and wood sealed with resistant finishes. Floors in areas used for food storage and utensil washing, walk-in refrigerators, and rest rooms should meet the same standards as those in food preparation areas.

Carpet is not allowed in areas where food is prepared or where equipment and utensils are washed because carpets are difficult to clean. Carpeting is used **only** in dining areas. When carpeting is used, it should be closely woven and easily cleanable.

Facilities that use sawdust, wood shavings, peanut hulls, or similar material as a floor covering are difficult to maintain. Consult your state and local rules and regulations for approved floor coverings.

Maintenance

All floors must be easy to clean and maintained in good repair.

- Antislip floor coverings should be used where they are needed for safety. Floor mats should be of nonabsorbent, grease-resistant materials that are easy to clean.

- Floor coverings should be properly installed so they do not cause accidents.

- Floors that are regularly cleaned with water or where water is spilled from sinks and dishwashers should be sealed and in good repair. Coving creates a curved, sealed edge between the floor and wall which makes cleaning easier and eliminates hiding places for insects.

- Properly installed floor drains with traps should exist in areas where liquids are often spilled. Floor drains make cleaning easier for floors that require scrubbing and help to get rid of big spills or overflows.

- Mats should be nonabsorbent and easy to clean. Clean them on a regular basis to prevent dirt buildup.

Utilities

Light fixtures, vent covers, wall-mounted fans, decorative materials, and similar equipment attached to walls and ceilings should be easy to clean and kept in good repair.

Plumbing fixtures must not interfere with proper cleaning of floors, walls, or ceilings.

Electrical wires and plumbing pipes should not be exposed in food handling or storage areas.

Lighting

It is important to have enough bright light where foods are handled and prepared. Poor lighting makes it harder to see dirt when cleaning the facility. When dirt can be seen, it is easier to clean and sanitize equipment, utensils, food contact surfaces, and all parts of the work area. Good lighting allows food workers to read and identify labels and colors and to inspect the condition of foods during storage, preparation, and serving.

Light bulbs located over or within food storage, preparation, and service areas, equipment, and utensil cleaning and storage areas should be shielded, coated, or otherwise shatter resistant.

Infrared or other heat lamps must also have covers. Shields should be around and extended beyond the face of the bulb, leaving only the face of the bulb exposed.

There are usually specific light intensity requirements for different areas of the food service establishment. Check with your local health department for specifics.

Heating, Air Conditioning, and Ventilation

Heating and Air Conditioning

Temperature control in food facilities takes careful planning and regulating. Heating systems and air conditioning may be needed to provide good working conditions. Foods must be kept at the correct temperatures during preparation and serving.

Ventilation

Ventilation removes smoke, odors, moisture, and greasy vapor and brings in fresh air. A good ventilating system should do the following:

- Carry away cooking vapors that could condense on walls and ceilings

- Make cleaning and maintenance easier by reducing the amount of dirt and grease

- Protect employee health by carrying away smoke and dirty air during cleaning or food preparation

- Provide a better work environment for employees by removing heat and cooking odors

All rooms with odors, vapors, or fumes should be vented to the outside. This includes all areas where cooking, frying, grilling, and dishwashing take place. All other rooms should have good ventilation to prevent heat, steam, condensation, vapors, bad smells, smoke, and fumes.

- Air vents for the ventilating system should be of the right size and located where they work well without causing drafts.

- Vents should be installed and operated according to state rules and must not cause fire hazards.

- Exhaust fumes vented to the outside should not bother the neighborhood or create dirty, harmful, or unlawful discharge.

- Intake and exhaust air ducts should be kept free of dust, dirt, insects, and other contaminants.

- When filters are used (unless they are designed to be cleaned in place) they must be easy to take out. Filters should be cleaned as often as needed (usually at least once a week).

- Ventilation hoods should be kept in good working order. Clean and inspect them regularly for buildups of dust and grease. Hoods should be cleaned as often as needed. Cleaning schedules should be set up and carried out as planned.

Outdoor Maintenance

Careful planning and maintenance of the areas outside the food service establishment is also important.

- Outside areas, including where the trash is stored, should be kept free from litter and old, unused equipment.

- Areas where customers walk should be level and smooth to make cleaning easy. Safety is a primary consideration.

- Driveways should be covered with concrete, asphalt, gravel, or similar material that is treated to keep down dust.

- All outdoor areas should be sloped so that water does not collect in pools.

Water and Plumbing

Water Supply

Potable water should be transported, handled, and dispensed in a sanitary manner. Unsafe water can cause disease by contaminating food, equipment, utensils, and hands. For the protection of customers and employees, you should only get potable water from sources that are regulated by law.

The work of a food service establishment depends on a steady supply of potable water. Water is used in all areas of food preparation and service, including:

- Hand washing

- Washing, spraying, dipping, and soaking produce

- Preparing and cooking foods

- Cleaning and sanitizing of equipment and utensils

- Ice making

- Preparing beverages

- Storing certain dispensing utensils that are in use (for example, dipper wells for ice cream scoops)

- Grinding garbage

- Thawing frozen foods

- Flushing toilets

You may be able to work around some short shutdowns in the water supply, such as those caused by water rationing plans or routine plumbing maintenance. If you have advance notice or if you know that the interruption will be short, you can obtain potable water from another place. You may be able to resort to stop-gap measures, such as using disposable tableware and kitchenware or substituting canned or frozen produce, when it is impossible to wash fresh fruits and vegetables.

However, you cannot continue operations if there is a plumbing failure, fire department demand for water, contamination, or if a natural disaster cuts off or endangers the water supply. If the safety of food, the cleanliness of utensils and equipment, and the personal hygiene of employees is in danger, food service must be halted. Contact the local health authorities immediately for advice when you are without water.

Water that is pure enough for drinking is called *potable water*. Potable water is required for all cleaning and sanitizing as well as for food production and drinking. Enough potable water for the needs of the food service establishment must come from a source constructed and operated according to law.

Nonpotable (not fit to drink) water is permitted **ONLY** for air conditioning and fire protection, and only if the system is installed according to law. The nonpotable water must not contact food or drip on food contact surfaces, utensils, or equipment that contacts food, and the piping must be separate from potable water and labeled as nonpotable.

Water hardness is an important factor. Hard water contains higher levels of minerals, which leave deposits on equipment and utensils and make general cleaning more difficult. If hard water is used, be sure washing, rinsing, and sanitizing procedures are done well.

Potable water that is not provided directly by pipe from a community water supply should be transported in a bulk water-transport system and delivered into a closed water system. Both of these systems should be constructed and operated according to law.

Bottled and packaged potable water should be bought from approved suppliers. It should be handled and stored in a way that protects it from contamination and should be used directly from the original container.

If an individual well is used as a source of water, it must meet all local construction standards. It must be inspected and sampled regularly by the authorities to make sure the water is clean and safe.

Plumbing

Water under pressure should be provided to all fixtures and equipment that use water. Hot and cold water should be available for cleaning and sanitizing of equipment and utensils, for cleaning of the physical facilities, and for proper employee hand washing. Pipes must be constructed of sturdy, leakproof materials.

Construction codes exist for plumbing systems. You should check with local authorities to be sure that the plumbing pipes are of the right size and that they are installed and maintained according to law.

Plumbing that is poorly installed or maintained can create sanitation hazards such as leaks and cross-connections. These conditions can cause the contamination of food, utensils, and equipment. Poor plumbing may also be a problem for equipment such as dishwashing machines and garbage grinders that depend on a sufficient amount of water and enough pressure to operate correctly.

Leakage

The location of plumbing pipes is important. Food preparation and service areas should never be located under overhead water pipes. If there is a leak, food, utensils, and equipment might be contaminated. Condensation of water on the outside of pipes can drip onto food or food preparation areas and contaminate food.

Cross-connection

Potable water should not mix with nonpotable or questionable water. In other words, there should be no cross-connections. Plumbing for nonpotable water must be separate and clearly marked. There must be no connections of potable water with any sources of contamination, such as drains, sewers, and waste pipes. Backflow, the flow of unsafe water into the supply of potable water, must be avoided.

Back Siphonage

Back siphonage can happen when pressure in the potable water supply drops below that of a non-potable, used, or contaminated water source.

An air gap is the best way to prevent back siphonage. An air gap is an open, vertical space between a supply of potable water and any possible source of contamination. An air gap of at least twice the diameter of the water supply inlet must be provided between the inlet and the flood-level rim of fixtures, equipment, and sinks. [A backflow or back-siphonage prevention device installed on a water supply system must meet American Society of Sanitary Engineers (ASSE) standards for construction, installation, and maintenance for the specific application of the type of device.]

When the drainage of fixtures or equipment does not have an air gap to prevent backflow or back siphonage, devices must be installed to protect the water supply. A hose should not be attached to a faucet unless a vacuum breaker is installed. For example, when the water pressure drops, contaminated water can enter the hose and flow into the potable water supply if a vacuum breaker is not in place.

Sinks and Drains

For effective manual washing, rinsing, and sanitizing of utensils and equipment, the sink must have at least three compartments. Sink compartments should be large enough to immerse the largest equipment and utensils. Each compartment of the sink should be supplied with hot and cold potable running water and should be properly connected to the drainage system. Sinks should have drainboards or easily movable dish tables, so that dirty utensils and equipment are kept separated from those that have been cleaned and sanitized. If drainboards are used, they must slope toward the sink.

- If grease traps or garbage grinders are used, they should be designed and located so that they are easy to clean.

- Grease traps should never fill to the top, and should be checked and cleaned on a regular basis.

- Air gaps must be used on all food preparation and food handling equipment (including ice machines). Air gaps should be at least twice the diameter of the water supply inlet but not less than 1 inch in diameter.

Floor drains with traps should be installed wherever water or liquid waste might build up. These areas include the following:

- Where sewage might overflow

- In rest rooms

- Where floors are water-flushed for cleaning

- Where water or liquid waste from equipment runs out

- Where equipment is cleaned with pressure spray methods

Sewage

Poor disposal of sewage may cause contamination of food, utensils, and equipment and may result in serious outbreaks of disease. Good drains help keep ground surfaces and water supplies clean and keep insects and other pests out.

All sewage, including liquid waste such as mop water, should flow into a public sewer system or a disposal system constructed and operated according to law. Sewage must be carried away by water, except in certain temporary food service establishments, in remote areas, or in special situations when permitted by local authorities.

Any problem with the sewage system is a serious hygiene hazard. If problems occur, you must check with the county health department and stop all food service operations if there is any risk to public health.

Garbage and Refuse

Storage

One way to prevent bad smells and pest infestation is by storing and disposing of garbage and refuse the right way. This will reduce the risk of contamination of food preparation and service areas.

•   Keep storage areas clean and in good repair.

•   Make sure that insects and rodents cannot get into the garbage.

•   Store refuse in covered containers, unless it consists only of cardboard, packaging, or materials that do not contain food wastes.

•   Bag all garbage before depositing in containers or dumpster.

•   Use rooms and areas—whether indoors or outside the building—that are large enough to hold all the containers needed.

•   Place containers, dumpsters, and compactor systems for outside use on a hard nonabsorbent surface. This hard surface should slope to drain.

Disposal

Garbage and refuse should be picked up often enough to prevent odors and to avoid attracting insects and rodents. Incineration is not a good way to dispose of garbage because garbage contains too much moisture to burn properly. If refuse is burned on the premises, it should be done by controlled incineration in accordance with federal and local laws and clean-air standards. Areas around incinerators should be clean and neat.

Containers

There should be enough containers to hold all garbage and refuse.

•   Use sturdy, easy-to-clean, insect- and rodent-proof containers that do not leak or absorb liquids. Plastic bags and wet-strength paper bags may be used to line containers.

•   Keep containers covered with tight-fitting lids.

•   Empty the containers used in food preparation and utensil washing areas as often as possible.

- Garbage containers, dumpsters, compactors, and compactor systems should be easy to clean and should have tight-fitting lids, doors, or covers.

- All containers must be in good shape and minimize waste liquid drainage. In containers designed with drains, drain plugs should always be in place, except during cleaning.

- Clean each container in a way that does not contaminate food, equipment, utensils, or food preparation areas. Facilities for washing containers should have hot water, detergent, or steam, and a floor drain. Each container, room, or area must be cleaned well after the garbage pickup. Liquid waste from compacting or cleaning operations must be disposed of as sewage. Do not throw this water on the ground.

Separate Facilities

Dressing Areas for Workers

Street clothes and personal belongings can carry contamination to food, equipment, and preparation surfaces. Having employees change from street clothing to uniforms or work clothing when they arrive at work can help reduce sanitation problems. If this is the policy, special rooms or areas must be made available for this purpose.

Lockers or closets should be provided for storing employees' belongings, such as purses, coats, shoes, and other personal articles, during the workday. Lockers or dressing rooms must not be located in areas where food is prepared or served or where utensils and equipment are cleaned. If absolutely necessary, lockers may be in rooms where completely packaged food or packaged single-service articles are stored.

Rooms used as living or sleeping quarters may not be used for food service operations. There cannot be a direct opening between the living area and the food service establishment.

Rest Rooms and Hand-Washing Facilities

Hands are probably the most common carriers of contamination to food and food contact surfaces. During normal operations, hands are exposed to a variety of contaminants. They must be washed well and often during the working day, after any interruption of the work routine, and after each visit to the toilet.

Facilities

Encourage employees to wash their hands well and often by setting up proper sinks and keeping them available at all times.

- Consult health authorities to learn how many sinks and toilets are required for your establishment.

- Equip each sink with hot and cold water mixed through a valve or combination faucet.

- Be sure that any self-closing, slow-closing, or metering faucets provide a flow of water for at least 15 seconds.

- Enclose rest rooms completely. Use tight-fitting, self-closing, solid doors, which should be kept closed except during cleaning or maintenance. Toilet rooms should not open directly into food preparation areas.

- Select toilets, urinals, and toilet fixtures that are designed to be easily cleaned and sanitized.

- All women's rest rooms must have a covered receptacle in each separate stall at all times.

Consult local authorities about the type of rest room facility needed for the handicapped according to the Americans with Disabilities Act, public law 101-336.

Supplies

Well-supplied rest rooms and sinks will encourage cleanliness. Hot and cold running water must be available at all times. An adequate supply of soap or detergent must be available at each hand-washing station. Forced-air blowers, paper towels, or rolled cloth towel dispensers must be used for hand drying. **DO NOT** use cloth towels that are used by more than one person.

- Place easily cleanable wastebaskets, which employees do not need to touch, at convenient locations.

- Stock all toilets with a good supply of toilet tissue at all times.

- Keep all toilets, soap dispensers, hand-drying devices, and related fixtures clean and in good repair.

Laundry Facilities

Laundry facilities in a food service establishment should be used only for washing and drying linens, cloths, uniforms, and aprons necessary for operation of the establishment.

- Keep laundry facilities away from food preparation areas and from other cleaning operations. Laundry may be done in storage rooms that contain packaged foods or packaged single-service articles, but a separate room is better.

- Store dirty clothes and linens in nonabsorbent containers or washable laundry bags until removed for laundering. Do not store these items in food storage units or on food contact surfaces.

- Protect clean uniforms and linens during storage.

Storing Hazardous Materials

Poisonous or toxic materials must be stored so that they do **not** contaminate food, equipment, utensils, linens, and single-service articles by:

- Separating the toxic materials by spacing or partitioning

- Locating the toxic materials in an area that is not above food, equipment, utensils, linens, and single-service articles

It is best to keep all poisonous or toxic materials out of the food preparation and serving areas unless they are absolutely necessary.

Only those poisonous or toxic materials that are required for the operation and maintenance of a food establishment, such as for cleaning and sanitizing of equipment and utensils and the control of insects and rodents, should be allowed in a food establishment. These materials include:

- Detergents, sanitizers, and other items used for cleaning and sanitizing

- Caustics, acids, polishes, and other chemicals used for maintenance

- Insecticides and rodenticides

Summary

As a manager, you need to know that your food service establishment must meet federal, state, and local health standards. Health inspectors have specific criteria that must be satisfied. Your job is to know what is expected, to anticipate problems, and to change practices whenever necessary to assure the safety of food, employees, and customers.

Chapter 8 Review Questions

1.   In what areas is carpeting allowed in a food service establishment?

2.   Why is it important to have sufficient lighting in the food preparation area?

3.   What is the definition of potable water?

4.   Nonpotable water can only be used for:

      A.

      B.

5.   An _____ is used to prevent back siphonage and should be located on all food preparation and food handling equipment with a liquid disposal system.

6.   How should used mop water be discarded?

7.   How often should garbage containers be cleaned?

See Appendix E for answers.

CHAPTER 9
Safety and Accident Prevention

☞ To protect themselves and the public, food service workers must follow safe procedures when they are on the job.

Preventing Accidents

An important part of your job is to make sure that the workplace is safe for employees. You must teach them how to avoid accidents. Every employee needs to be trained in proper procedures to use, operate and clean equipment. To avoid accidents, you must observe the employees at work to make sure that they are being careful.

Safety Procedures

Make sure all workers understand that they can help to prevent accidents by doing tasks carefully. The following are a few of the practices that will help to reduce the risks for both customers and employees.

To Prevent Falls

- Keep floors and floor mats clean, dry, in good repair, and free of trash and other obstacles.

- Wipe up spills immediately.

- Follow the manufacturer's instructions for using floor cleaners. Rinse thoroughly after mopping to prevent the floors from being slippery due to detergent or grease film.

- After cleaning or mopping floors, use "caution" or "wet floor" signs.

- Use slip-resistant floor coverings or products that reduce sliding.

- Employees' shoes should always be slip-resistant.

- Provide adequate lighting in all areas.

- Use a safe, well-placed ladder or stool for climbing—NOT a chair, box, or shelf.

- DO NOT run. Always look where you are walking.

- Mark stairs carefully and provide handrails.

- Keep drawers and cabinets closed when not in use.

- Store materials properly so that people do not fall over them.

- Do not clutter work areas or floors with unnecessary utensils or supplies.

- Use carts and handcarts to transport heavy objects from place to place.

- Instruct employees in correct lifting and storing methods (provide a safety belt).

To Prevent Burns

- Remove lids from pots, pans, and kettles carefully, allowing steam to escape away from the face and hand.

- Check pots and pans to make sure the handles are sturdy.

- Use dry, flameproof potholders.

- Turn the handles of pans inward on the range so that pans cannot be knocked off. Make sure that handles are not placed too near the heat.

- Move heavy or hot containers with enough help and know where the containers are going before picking them up.

- Operate coffee urns and other hot beverage machines as the manufacturer suggests.

- Be aware of the hot edges of ranges, ovens, and broilers. Do not allow running or playing near such equipment.

- Be careful when filtering or changing shortening in fryers. Wear gloves and aprons for protection.

- To avoid flash fires, do not place frozen foods with large ice crystals on the surface of the item into the hot shortening in deep fryers.

- To avoid burns from heat lamps, place caution signs on heated counters and serving areas.

- Keep stove tops and hoods free of grease.

- Keep oven doors closed when not in use.

- Do not clean ovens and stoves until they have cooled.

- Keep papers, plastic aprons, and other flammable materials away from hot areas.

To Prevent Cuts

- Use the right knife for the job, and keep it sharp.

- Always cut away from the body, never toward it.

- Do not reach blindly for a knife.

- If a knife falls, don't grab it. Get out of the way.

- Use knives with built-in guards or shaped handles which give you a firmer grip. Use sharpening steels with the guard placed between the handle and steel.

- Wear protective mesh gloves and cuff guards when using knives all the time and when taking meat slicers apart for cleaning.

- Keep all sharp knives in a knife holder. When knives are stored in drawers, place them in a rack.

- Wash all sharp tools separately from other utensils.

- Use the proper tools for the job. Do not use knives as screwdrivers, can openers, or box openers.

- Throw out broken utensils and replace damaged equipment.

- To prevent cuts, throw out broken glass in special containers.

Handling Special Equipment

The specialized equipment used in many food service operations can be dangerous if not used properly. **Turn the switch to the OFF position and disconnect the power before removing food or cleaning any machine.**

Cutters and Choppers

- Be sure that all parts are properly installed and that the safety guards are in place before operating these machines.

- Use a rubber or plastic spatula to remove food.

- Store blades and other parts so that accidental cuts or contamination do not occur.

Slicers

- Keep hands away from the blade.

- Follow special safety procedures for machines with a power feed.

- When cleaning a slicer, protect your hands with cut-resistant mesh gloves.

- Follow the manufacturer's recommendations and instructions when cleaning any machine.

Grinders

- When working with food grinders, use a feed stomper and keep all guards in place while the machine is in use.

- Keep fingers away from the feed screw. Grinders with small feed necks are usually safer.

- Turn the grinder off, disconnect the power, and wait until the machine comes to a complete stop before adjusting or cleaning.

Disposal Units

- Do not use tampers, hands, or other devices in food disposals.

- Use a guard so that silverware does not get into the disposal.

- Turn off the machine before removing trapped metal or cloths.

First Aid

Preparing for Emergencies

You may face many emergencies in the day-to-day operation of a food establishment, ranging from simple accidents to life-threatening events. Minor accidents often require that first aid be administered right away. Victims of more serious accidents and injuries need qualified medical treatment, but they may need immediate first-aid care before help arrives. Know what to do and have the equipment to do it. You can help to avoid needless suffering and perhaps save a life.

Post the telephone numbers for emergency services, including doctors, the fire department, ambulances, poison control, and the health department near the phone. KEEP A FIRST-AID KIT WITH INSTRUCTIONS ON WHAT TO DO IN A HANDY PLACE. Store the kit so as to prevent the contamination of food, equipment, utensils, linens, and single-service articles. The general first-aid guidelines on the following pages are no substitute for a current first-aid manual. Organizations such as the American Red Cross or a local hospital can help provide references and first-aid training for all who work in your establishment.

Be prepared for emergencies and remain calm. An injured worker must not handle food again until the wound is properly treated.

General Guidelines for Giving First Aid

Procedures should be clearly defined and understood. Employees who know what to do in emergencies are valuable resources in your establishment. The following points should be included in your plan and instructions.

•   Stay calm. When an accident occurs, information is needed to find out how serious the problem may be.

•   Quickly decide whether or not to call for help—if in doubt, call. Posted telephone numbers speed up the process.

•   Make the accident victim as comfortable as possible until help arrives or a minor injury is treated.

•   Administer first aid according to the type of problem—cuts, burns, falls, etc. Consult your first-aid guide for instructions.

•   Control the situation by keeping away from the victim anyone not needed to help.

•   Write down the victim's name, the date and time of accident, type of injury or illness, treatment, and how long it took for any assistance such as emergency medical services, fire department, or hospital ambulance to arrive. This information will be needed by management and insurance company adjustors.

First-Aid Supplies

Keep first-aid supplies in a clearly marked box in an easy-to-find place near, but not in, the food preparation area. Each workstation should have a first-aid kit nearby. Show employees where the first-aid kit is kept.

Cuts, burns, sprains, and bruises are the most common forms of injury in restaurants. Local fire departments, hospital emergency rooms, and American Red Cross chapters have information on what supplies should be kept and where to obtain simple instructions for first-aid treatment. All supplies in the kit should be labeled and expiration dates checked each month so that outdated items can be replaced.

Burns

Burns are serious injuries that require immediate treatment. Deciding how severe a burn is should be done by a qualified medical professional.

General principles in first-aid treatment of burns include the following:

- Stop the burning process by removing whatever caused the burning.

- Use cool, running water to soothe MINOR burns.

- DO NOT APPLY OINTMENTS, SPRAYS, ANTISEPTICS, or HOME REM-EDIES.

- Keep the victim calm and quiet.

- Seek medical assistance immediately when it is indicated by the size and severity of the burn.

The cause of the burn, amount of skin affected, and whether or not flames may have been breathed in by the victim all contribute to the type of care that should be given. Therefore, get help as soon as possible. Burns are classified as first degree (reddening), second degree (blisters), and third degree (charring).

Burns of the hands, feet, face, and groin area are considered serious and should be checked by professional medical personnel. Call your emergency medical system number, fire department, or hospital emergency room for instructions on what should be done. Many areas have a 911 telephone emergency system, which can speed up the response of the correct unit to help with the emergency.

Choking

An alert employee WHO KNOWS WHAT TO DO may be able to save the life of a person who is choking by using the Heimlich maneuver. Having employees trained in cardiopulmonary resuscitation (CPR) techniques is also a good idea but not required.

You may post a sign illustrating the Heimlich maneuver in an easily visible place. Getting instruction to teach employees how to use the Heimlich maneuver is desirable but not required. The American Red Cross will provide the signs to post in your establishment.

The law does not require a public food service establishment or employee to provide emergency assistance, but it does not forbid taking action. No establishment or employee will be held liable for civil damages for an action that could be expected of any reasonably prudent person under similar circumstances.

Wounds

Glassware, sharp utensils, and slicing equipment are needed to prepare and serve food, but food workers who continually handle these articles risk getting cut. Cuts and other wounds require immediate attention.

First Aid for Minor Cuts

- Rinse in clean running water.

- Apply pressure with a clean towel or napkin.

- Get a first-aid kit.

- Follow the instructions provided in the kit.

- Apply a water-resistant bandage, covered by a plastic glove if a hand is involved.

- All severe cuts and punctures should be treated by a medical professional.

Reporting Accidents

When an accident has occurred, the food establishment manager or supervisor should write a report of the accident, what happened, and the emergency assistance response for use by the insurance company. Workers' Compensation programs, the Occupational Safety and Health Administration (OSHA), and the establishment's own insurance company will supply forms for filing an accident report.

The accident report is sent to the appropriate party. The insurance company will examine the report and may investigate further. The company will arrange a settlement that is consistent with state compensation laws.

Fire Safety

Fire Prevention

Fires cause property damage. They can also lead to serious accidents and even death. Fires can be prevented by good work habits. If a fire does occur, a quick, trained reaction can reduce damage and save lives.

All employees must work together to prevent fires in food service establishments. However, *you* have the final responsibility for fire safety. Make sure that the following rules are followed by all workers and remember that keeping the workplace neat and clean helps to prevent the chance of fires.

- Remind your employees to "think fire safety."

- Gas appliances can be dangerous if not properly maintained. A buildup of escaped gas can create an explosion if a match is lit for any reason.

- When clearing ashtrays used by customers and employees, be certain that all cigarettes and cigars are out.

- Oily rags must be stored in properly designed metal cans.

- All smoke alarms and protection equipment must be properly installed and maintained.

- Grease to be thrown out should not pile up in the workplace.

- All appliances and equipment must be installed properly.

- All flammable and combustible materials must be stored away from any heat source.

- Never allow burnable material to pile up under stairways or near electric motors, ranges, ovens, or water heaters.

- Always put waste paper and rubbish in the proper containers.

- Make sure that waste containers are removed from the kitchen when full, and that they are promptly replaced with clean empty containers.

- Check all equipment power cords for damage on a regular basis.

- Do not splash water next to electrical outlets.

- Clean hoods and exhaust filters over cooking equipment often (at least weekly), especially after a lot of grilling. The buildup of grease in these areas creates a fire hazard.

- Clean hood ductwork a minimum of twice a year using a professional cleaning company.

- Smoke only in designated areas. All smoking products must be put out and thrown away safely.

- Tableside cooking can be quite dangerous. If permitted in your establishment by state and local authorities, special care must be taken to ensure that nobody will get hurt. This includes keeping the cooking area clear and free of combustibles and using a heat-resistant surface under the cooking device. Be especially careful not to add a flammable liquid to an open flame, to prevent a flashback.

- All propane storage, if used in your establishment, must be approved by authorities.

Types of Fires

Four things must be present for an unplanned and uncontrolled fire to occur: a heat source, oxygen, a flammable or combustible material, and a dangerous act. Fires are classified according to the nature of the material that catches fire.

*   Class A fires occur in ordinary combustible materials such as wood, paper, cloth, and many plastics. Such fires may occur throughout a food service operation, particularly in storerooms, dining rooms, and garbage areas.

*   Class B fires occur in flammable liquids and grease—most frequently in kitchens and maintenance areas.

*   Class C fires involve live electrical equipment, such as in motors, transformers, and similar equipment.

Types of Fire Extinguishers

Different types of extinguishers use different chemicals and are used for different types of fires. Each type must be installed in the correct area.

A Class A fire—regular wood or paper, etc.—requires use of a Class A extinguisher. A Class B fire—grease and oil—requires use of a Class B extinguisher. A Class C fire—electrical—requires use of a Class C extinguisher.

The different-shaped symbols displayed below indicate the different types of extinguishers. Check extinguisher tags for symbols to determine what type of fire they were designed to extinguish. There are combination extinguishers that can be used for more than one type of fire.

Class	Symbol	Color
Class A Wood, Paper	△ A	Green
Class B Grease, Oil	☐ B	Red
Class C Electrical	◯ C	Blue

Installing Fire Extinguishers

Always consult local authorities when you are installing or checking your equipment. You must comply with specific state laws concerning the number of extinguishers, the types required, their placement, and their maintenance.

Local authorities are always willing to offer demonstrations on the proper use of fire extinguishers. All employees must know how to use an extinguisher before a fire occurs. Since many fire extinguishers release all of their extinguishing agent in just a few seconds, there is no time to experiment when a fire breaks out. Most extinguishers have a locking mechanism such as a ring pin to prevent accidental discharge. Everyone must know how to squeeze the trigger and discharge the extinguisher. Local fire departments can demonstrate how to use fire extinguishers and provide other related information if requested.

Fire extinguishers must be checked from time to time and properly maintained. Be sure that they have not been discharged or tampered with, and that they are not damaged. You must recharge most types of extinguishers every 6 months. The state conducts regular maintenance inspections to certify extinguishers as operable.

- Fire extinguishers must be labeled and tagged. Their location should be clearly marked with a wall sign.

- Put signs on walls or columns to indicate the location of fire extinguishers.

- Review frequently the proper use of extinguishers.

- Inspect extinguishers yourself between the official state inspections.

- Always replace or recharge extinguishers after use.

- Extinguishers must be hydrostatically tested every 5 years.

- Maximum distances between extinguishers must comply with local law.

Fire extinguishers must be near the job and easy to see. They must be stored properly. If an extinguisher weighs less than 40 pounds, it may not be mounted more than 5 feet off the ground. If it weighs more than 40 pounds, it may not be mounted more than 3.5 feet off the ground. No extinguisher may be stored less than 4 inches from the ground.

Other Fire Protection Equipment

Hood Systems

Food service establishments should be properly ventilated to remove greasy vapors, as well as excess heat and smoke. The system should be inspected according to local fire codes. Usually, these ventilation systems are called hood systems. Hood systems are commonly installed over cooking equipment and dishwashers. Not only do these systems remove vapors, heat, and smoke, but they also have some type of fire extinguishing agent and sprinkler system installed as well. Grease trays should be installed above the food preparation area and cleaned on a routine schedule. Your employees should be taught the use of these extinguishing systems. The hood system must be installed by a professional and maintained on a regular schedule.

Sprinkler Systems

Many new buildings are required by local law to have a sprinkler system installed. If you have such a system, be sure to keep supplies the regulated distance away from each sprinkler head and equipment. Sprinkler heads must be clean. If a sprinkler head is knocked off, contact a professional immediately.

Emergency Procedures in Case of Fire

Panic by customers and employees when a fire breaks out can make fire protection equipment useless and can increase the danger to human life. All employees must know fire extinguisher locations, the emergency telephone numbers, and who to contact.

- Plan and practice evacuation procedures so that all employees know the emergency exit routes and doors.

- Post in easy-to-see places diagrams of the escape route, together with any other information that will assist in an orderly evacuation.

- Train new employees in these procedures when they begin work and hold periodic refresher sessions for all workers.

The following is a sample emergency procedure:

- Call the fire department as soon as a fire is discovered, even if it appears that you can put it out yourselves with portable equipment.

- Let all employees know about the fire.

- Move all customers and employees out of the building.

- Emphasize the employees' role in calmly helping in the evacuation of customers, who will not know where emergency exits are located or how to get to them.

- Keep all exits accessible and unlocked on the inside at all times and do not block or obstruct them at any time.

- Life safety must be the most important concern of all food service employees.

Fire Inspectors

Fire inspectors will conduct inspections in your establishment to see if you are following all fire safety regulations.

Summary

As manager or supervisor in a food service establishment, the safety of yourself, employees, and customers is your responsibility. Procedures to assist you, well-trained employees, and good common sense are needed in emergency situations. By following a routine schedule of monitoring safety procedures and training staff, you will be prepared to act if the need should arise.

Chapter 9 Review Questions

1. State three ways to prevent an accident in the following categories:

    A. To prevent falls

        1.

        2.

        3.

    B. To prevent burns

        1.

        2.

        3.

    C. To prevent cuts

        1.

        2.

        3.

    D. To prevent a fire

        1.

        2.

        3.

2. Where would you place a first-aid kit?

3. What would you do if an employee received a burn of the hands, feet, or face?

4. Identify the three types of fires by combustible material type and by classification letter, symbol, and color of extinguisher type.

    A.

    B.

    C.

See Appendix E for answers.

CHAPTER 10
Training

By teaching food safety and practices, principles of providing safe food, and making sure that employees know how to protect themselves and others on the job, both time and money can be saved. Furthermore, it is a joy for any manager to work in a food service establishment where everyone is well-trained and motivated to serve food that is safe to eat.

Responsibilities

Managers and supervisors of food service establishments are responsible for the way food handlers and employees perform their jobs. High employee turnover makes a continuous and consistent training program very important.

The major causes of foodborne illness are procedural. In other words, the wrong method of handling a product can cause the food to be contaminated before it is served. Potentially hazardous foods held at inadequate product temperatures continue to be the primary problem that produces foodborne illness.

If procedures and a lack of knowledge are the problem, proper training should be the solution. The extra cost and effort of training can be justified by the return gained by avoiding a foodborne outbreak of illness or employee injury.

To achieve the goal of having a well-trained staff, the following ingredients have to be present.

- **KNOWLEDGE** of basic food safety and correct procedures

- **MOTIVATION** to do the right thing at the right time

- A **WORKPLACE** where good policies and procedures are expected and encouraged

Analyzing the Job to Be Learned

An important part of the manager's job description is training. The actual training may be done by someone else, but final responsibility rests with the manager.

To do a task analysis you must look at a particular job and divide it into small tasks. Write down each task in the order in which they should be performed. By having a written record of the steps or tasks involved, both the new employee and the person who is doing the training will know exactly what is expected.

Training is usually done by pairing a new employee with a trained employee who already knows how to do the job. The question to ask is: Do employees learn the correct procedures this way, or are bad habits being passed from one employee to another? Without some kind of written task analysis, or some description of how to do a job correctly every time it is done, you cannot be sure of the outcome.

For example, if the new employee is to learn how to clean and sanitize equipment and utensils using a chemical sanitizer, list the tasks required to complete the job.

- Use a three-compartment sink.

- Clean and sanitize surfaces of the sink compartments before filling.

- Fill the first compartment with hot water (100 to 120°F).

- Add detergent in sufficient quantity to satisfy the manufacturer's instructions (directions on the container).

- Fill the second compartment with hot water for rinsing the detergent from the dishes after washing.

- Fill the third compartment with warm water (at least 75°F for chlorine) and add sanitizer according to the directions on the container.

Continue writing down the steps until they are all listed and the final product (clean and sanitized equipment and utensils) is achieved.

The list with all the steps needed to complete the job is called a *procedure* and can be used by all employees to make sure that the job is always done correctly and consistently.

Motivation

Motivating employees to learn requires the trainer to understand the needs of the employees. Following a list will help a trainer plan the training that will appeal to the employee and increase the chance that the information will be used.

Learning Principles

- **Motivation** to learn is critical. Employees need to feel that they will benefit from the training.

- Employees retain that which is **relevant** to them, especially practical skills needed to get the job done efficiently. If they see where they will apply the information, they will be motivated and learn better.

- Employees learn best by active **participation** in the learning process.

- Employees learn in **different** ways and at **varying speeds**.

- Employees will learn best if a **variety of training materials** are used. Everyone does not learn the same way. Use videos, audiotapes, posters, pictures, pamphlets, demonstrations, games, or any other method of presenting material which provides different ways to learn.

- **Reinforce learning** that is achieved by **praising** and giving **rewards**. The employee who is praised and/or rewarded for applying what he or she has learned gives incentive to other employees to improve their knowledge.

- Treat employees with **respect**. There is no such thing as a "dumb" question. If more information is needed, perhaps the meaning was not clear. Employees embarrass easily and need positive feedback to overcome feelings of inadequacy. Be candid with your audience. If you do not know the answer to a question, say so. Simply indicate that you will find the answer and report back.

- **Short** sessions (30 to 45 minutes) are most effective.

- All learners like **feedback** on their ability to apply what they have learned. Evaluate and inform learners of their progress.

- **Know the employees' level of knowledge** and present material in a way that they can easily understand. When employees know what is expected and how to do it, results are usually positive.

Trainers

Managers, supervisors, and trained employees usually provide the training in food service establishments. If the organization is large, corporate resources may be available in the form of trainers and learning materials. However, even if the materials and training outlines are already in place, you must know how to put them to use. Knowing the material yourself is the first requirement. It is impossible to teach what you do not fully understand yourself, and once credibility is lost, it is hard to regain. If you assign someone else to do the training, the final responsibility for the information is still yours.

There are resources in your community that can be called upon to help train employees. Local health departments can help in sanitation training. The American Red Cross supplies first-aid training, Heimlich maneuver, and cardiopulmonary resuscitation (CPR) instruction. Your local fire department can supply a fire extinguisher demonstration, plus other information on how to handle fire emergencies. Your state agricultural extension service also provides training materials and training in the area of food sanitation and safety.

Developing a Training Plan

When there is a problem with contaminated food, wasted products, employee health or injury, an inspection, or a dissatisfied customer, the usual response is to conduct an educational session immediately. A "quick fix" may be needed to correct a problem, but the manager needs to learn from the bad experience and develop a training plan that will prevent every problem from becoming a crisis.

Evaluation

All employees deserve to know how they are performing. Once the needs are identified, the objectives are written, and the initial training and ongoing supervision are supplied, a change in actions should be noticeable. The entire training process is focused on the training of new employees and the improved performance of existing employees.

A short-term evaluation usually comes at the end of a training session when a student shows his or her ability in a demonstration or a written exercise. Long-term evaluation occurs when work habits demonstrate a favorable change.

Records of training received, classes taken, performance demonstrated, etc., are valuable tools when promotions, salary increases, or hiring/firing issues arise. The record can be a simple file box with an index card for each employee, with notes on training and performance. Larger organizations use printed forms.

Scheduling Training Sessions

In a busy food establishment, choosing the time and place for training is often difficult. Decide what the priorities of training are by checking reports from inspections or audits and observe employee practices to determine if there are problems that need immediate attention. Also address customer complaints and concerns that have been expressed. Set up the master schedule based on those identified needs. A lot of one-to-one training is done in food service establishments, but when you have to repeat the same training to several people, it will save time to handle them as a group.

The master training schedule can also be used to reinforce certain principles and practices that need periodic repetition and updating, such as sanitary food practices, fire safety, pest control information, or any other topic that employees need to know and remember. There will always be a need for special sessions on specific problems or events, so build some flexibility into your schedule.

Choose the method of instruction (one to one, groups by level and type of job, or the entire staff) according to the nature of the lesson to be learned and the number of people involved. There are times when one-to-one training is justified, but use it wisely. Regular training sessions that include the entire staff keep everyone informed and up to date on general issues. Sometimes, training programs that involve supervisory and staff together inhibit discussion. Classes can be held in the dining room, storage areas, or kitchen, depending on the subject being taught.

Summary

A training program is a good investment for a food service establishment. Savings gained from having well-trained employees dictate the time, money, and effort that go into a good training program. Managerial commitment to training is demonstrated when training is given priority treatment. Scheduling classes, posting dates in advance, and making sure that employees are able to attend the sessions send the message that training is valued.

Chapter 10 Review Questions

1. What three elements produce a well-trained staff?

    A.

    B.

    C.

2. What is a task analysis?

3. Why is it important to have a written task analysis of each job?

See Appendix E for answers.

CHAPTER 11
Federal, State, and Local Rules and Regulations

☞ *The purpose of governmental regulation in the food industry is to protect food served to the public. Since there are many opportunities for food to become contaminated from the time it is grown and harvested until it is consumed, the government (federal, state, and local) monitors both the process and the product to ensure the safety of food.*

Federal Regulatory Agencies

Regulation by the federal government focuses on the sources of food and protection of the products until they are purchased, processed, and consumed by the public.

Food and Drug Administration

The Food and Drug Administration's (FDA) activities are directed toward protecting the health of the nation against impure and unsafe foods, drugs, and cosmetics, and other potential hazards. The FDA develops and enforces regulations with regards to the safety, composition, quality (including nutrition), and labeling of foods, food additives, colors, cosmetics, drugs, and medical devices.

At the federal level, the FDA is a resource for state and local agencies that require assistance in formulating codes and regulations. The FDA publishes documents related to food service sanitation and enforces mandatory provisions of laws and regulations concerning food service operations by interstate carriers. The FDA also publishes lists of food additives and the amounts allowed in food products.

The most recent publication for guidance in the food service industry is the Food Code, published by the FDA, US. Department of Health and Human Services.

U.S. Department of Agriculture

The U.S. Department of Agriculture (USDA) benefits all Americans on a daily basis. The USDA works to improve food production and strives to cure poverty, hunger, and malnutrition. It also works to protect the soil, water, forests, and other natural resources. Furthermore, the USDA, through its inspection and grading services, safeguards and ensures standards of quality in the daily food supply.

Inspection of food processing plants and supervision of labeling practices is shared by the U.S. Department of Agriculture and the FDA. The USDA inspects meat, meat products, poultry, poultry products, eggs, egg products, dairy products, fruits, and vegetables.

Centers for Disease Control

The Centers for Disease Control (CDC) is the federal agency charged with protecting the public health through the prevention and control of diseases and response to public health emergencies.

Foodborne illness is monitored by the CDC, which is located in Atlanta, Georgia. This agency is responsible for determining how an outbreak occurred and publishes statistical information about the incidence and severity of the illnesses. CDC also supplies educational materials about sanitation.

Environmental Protection Agency

The Environmental Protection Agency (EPA) protects and enhances our environment today and for future generations. The agency's mission is to control and battle pollution related to the air, water, solid waste, pesticides, radiation, and toxic substances. The EPA works with state and local governments in a coordinated attack on environmental pollution. It does research, monitoring, and standard setting and enforces antipollution activities.

National Marine Fisheries Service

The National Marine Fisheries Service (NMFS) of the U.S. Department of Commerce develops voluntary standards for the sanitary quality of fishing waters and processing methods.

Occupational Safety and Health Act

The Occupational Safety and Health Administration, (OSHA), which was established after the Occupational Safety and Health Act of 1970, develops and promotes occupational safety and health standards, develops and issues regulations, conducts investigations and inspections, and issues citations and proposes penalties for noncompliance with safety and health standards and regulations.

Employers are required by OSHA to provide employees with safe working conditions. OSHA sets standards for a hazard-free working environment, safe equipment, and job procedures with safety in mind.

Additional Organizations

Information and assistance with specific aspects of food safety may be obtained from the following organizations. Start a resource file with laws, codes, and materials that will help you have the knowledge you need to be a top-flight manager who knows the answers. Appendix A contains the addresses of most of these organizations or groups.

American Public Health Association (APHA)

Association of Food and Drug Officials (AFDO)

Food Marketing Institute (FMI)

Food Research Institute

Frozen Food Industry Coordinating Committee

International* Association of Milk, Food, and Environmental Sanitarians (IAMFES)

National Environmental Health Association (NEHA)

National Pest Control Association

National Restaurant Association (NRA)

National Shellfish Safety Program

NSF International (formerly known as the National Sanitation Foundation)

State Cooperative Extension Service

State and Local Regulations and Inspections

As a manager, the state and local regulations have the most effect on your establishment. You need to know and follow the state and local regulations and always be ready for inspections. Resisting inspections or challenging the results will not accomplish the real goal of programs that monitor compliance to rules that are made to protect the public.

Regulations

State and Local Laws

Environmental health specialists monitor the conditions of individual establishments to determine whether they are in compliance with state and local laws. A copy of the regulations should be obtained from your local public health department or from the county commission.

Managerial Responsibility

The sanitarian who inspects the food service establishment is checking to see if the rules and regulations are being followed. Lack of knowledge on the part of the manager does not excuse a deficiency. It is your responsibility to get copies of rules and regulations from the appropriate office and follow the rules in the food service establishment.

The food service manager must be aware of the purpose and function of the local registered sanitarian who conducts the inspections. When it is understood that the sanitarian is a valuable resource person and another set of eyes to help you serve safe food, you can work with the inspector to make your establishment one of the best. If self-inspections are conducted routinely and changes are made when needed, your work will pay off handsomely when the inspector arrives. If you and your employees follow an effective sanitation program, you will not have to worry about the inspector finding fault with critical items.

Managers should be aware of special laws and regulations, such as allowing Seeing Eye dogs (U.S. Code, 1982 Edition, Title 40, "Public Buildings, Property, and Works," Section 291) and police officers' guard dogs into dining areas. State statutes and federal rules for allowing the presence of live fish, shellfish, and crustaceans are provided in Appendix F.

Inspections

What Inspections Monitor

Food and supplies, personal hygiene and health of food handlers, equipment and utensils, sanitizing practices, facilities, water supply, waste disposal, and construction standards are all monitored for possible signs of contamination or lack of safety.

Using Self-Inspections to Prepare for Official Health Inspections

The manager, who is the person ultimately responsible, must be ready for inspections at all times. The purpose of inspection is to help maintain safe, sanitary establishments. The twice-a-year visit from an inspector is not going to solve your problems. By setting up self-inspections based on what must be in compliance, continuing to monitor the status, and making improvements as needed, you will always be prepared for a visit from the health inspector. However, the final benefit of self-inspection is the safe food served to customers.

A sample self-inspection report has been included at the end of this chapter.

Handling Official Inspections

When the inspector arrives, assist as needed. Be professional and courteous, and always be available for questions. Have the necessary records at hand to validate or explain what the inspector needs to know. A violation that is cited will be in the report given to you by the inspector. Acknowledge the problem and fix it immediately. Fines and possible closure of the establishment can result when warnings are not taken seriously. If you need more information about a problem or do not know how to fix it, ask the inspector for additional resources.

Foodborne Illness Outbreak (Two or More People with Same Symptoms)

When a foodborne illness outbreak occurs, you must stop serving food and call for help. Do not throw away any food since samples will have to be provided to the health department. They will also interview employees as the investigation proceeds. It is suggested that you keep a part of the sample taken by the inspector to use if another test is needed. Cooperate with the authorities. Their job is to find the problem. Your job is to correct the problem if it is within your scope of responsibility. For your protection you should keep all records from suppliers, preparation procedures, and employees involved. You may also wish to conduct your own investigation using an independent laboratory.

Summary

Government supervision of the food industries has become an important function in an increasingly complex world. To protect the public from contaminated food, many steps are required to monitor food before it reaches the food establishment, and ultimately when it is consumed by the public. Inspectors and inspections exist for your benefit, and you are encouraged to interact with the various health agencies to learn all you can about serving safe food and protecting the public. Use the assistance and materials that can be obtained from professional and trade organizations to help you solve problems and become a proactive manager. You are responsible for knowing and complying with all state and local rules and regulations.

Chapter 11 Review Questions

1.   What do the letters of each of the following organizations stand for?

   A.   FDA

   B.   USDA

   C.   CDC

   D.   EPA

   E.   OSHA

2.   Why would you do a self-inspection?

See Appendix E for answers.

Appendix A
Agency Addresses

Agencies Involved in Food Protection

The following are the addresses of some agencies involved in food protection. Each organization has learning materials specific to its area. Many publications and audiovisual aides are available from these sources.

American Public Health Association
1015 15th Street N.W.
Washington, DC 20005
(202) 789-5600

Association of Food and Drug Officials
P.O. Box 3425
York, PA 17402-3425
(717) 757-2888

Centers for Disease Control
1600 Clifton Road
Atlanta, GA 30333
(404) 639-2206

Culinary Institute of America
433 Albany Street
Hyde Park, NY 12538-1499
(914) 452-9600

Multiple titles available.
  Catalog available upon request.
  Multimedia.

Educational Institute of the American Hotel & Motel Association
1407 South Harrison Road
East Lansing, MI 48823
(517) 353-5500

Food Marketing Institute
800 Connecticut Avenue N.W.
Washington, DC 20006
(202) 452-8444

International Food Service Manufacturers Association
321 North Clark Street, Suite 2900
Chicago, IL 60610
(312) 644-8989

Milk Industry Foundation
888 16th Street N.W., 2nd Floor
Washington, DC 20006
(202) 296-4250

National Environment Health Association
720 South Colorado Boulevard, Suite 970
South Tower
Denver, CO 80222
(303) 756-9090

National Pest Control Association
8100 Oak Street
Loring, VA 22027
(703) 573-8330

National Restaurant Association
1200 17th Street N.W.
Washington, DC 20036-3097
1-800-424-5156
(202) 331-5900
Fax (202) 331-2429
8-minute videotape: *The AIDS Issue:
    Guidelines for Foodservice Managers*

**NSF International (formerly National
    Sanitation Foundation)**
3475 Plymouth Road
Ann Arbor, MI 48105
(313) 769-8010

Shellfish Institute of North America
1525 Wilson Boulevard, Suite 500
Arlington, VA 22209
(703) 524-8883

**U.S. Department of Health and Human
    Services**
Public Health Service
Food and Drug Administration
200 C Street S.W.
Washington, DC 20204

The Milk Safety Branch, HFF-346,
provides the "IMS List Sanitation Compliance
and Enforcement Ratings of Interstate Milk
Shippers."

The Shellfish Sanitation Branch, HFF0513,
provides the "Interstate Certified Shellfish
Shippers List."

General

American Red Cross—local chapter

Free pamphlet: *Your Job and Aids*

**FDA Center for Food Safety and Applied
    Nutrition**
200 C Street S.W.
Washington, DC 20204-0001
(202) 205-5251

Catalog of information materials for the food
    and cosmetic industries.

National Agricultural Chemical Association
1155 Fifteenth Street N.W., Suite 900
Washington, DC 20005
(202) 296-1585

National Audio-Visual Center
Customer Service Section PY
8700 Edgeworth Drive
Capitol Heights, MD 20743-3701
(301) 763-1896

Multiple titles available.

OSHA
Occupational Safety and Health Administration
200 Constitution Avenue, N.W., Room N-3101
Washington, DC 20210
1-800-424-5156
(202) 219-4667

Pamphlet OSHA-3102: *Worker Exposure to
    AIDS and Hepatitis B*

Additional Suggested Government Listings

U.S. Department of Agriculture
c/o Modern Talking Pictures
5000 Park Street North
St. Petersburg, FL 33709
(813) 541-7571

Videotape:
Food Safety Is No Mystery

U.S. Department of Agriculture
Food Safety and Inspection Service Informa-
  tion Office
South Agriculture Building
Independence Avenue S.W.
Washington, DC 20250
(202) 720-8732

Salmonella Bacteria and Salmonella Food
  Poisoning: Questions and Answers.
  Multiple materials available.

U.S. Food and Drug Administration,
Industry Guidance Branch (5425 FB8)
200 C Street S.W.
Washington, DC 20204
(202) 205-5251

U.S. Food and Drug Administration - Retail
  Food Protection Branch (HFF-342)
200 C Street S.W.
Washington, DC 20204-0001
(202) 205-8140

U.S. Food and Drug Administration
State Training Branch (HCF-153)
5600 Fishers Lane
Rockville, MD 20857
(301) 443-5871
FAX (301) 443-2143

Bibliography of Training Materials.

U.S. Government Printing Office
Superintendent of Documents
Washington, DC 20402-9325
(202) 783-3238

DHEW Publication (FDA) 78-2081:
Food Service Sanitation Manual
This manual is also available in Spanish. One
copy of the Spanish edition per organization
may be obtained at no cost.

Sources of Audiovisual Aids

Britannica Films
Encyclopedia Britannica
    Educational Corporation
425 North Michigan Avenue
Chicago, IL 60611

Coronet Films & Video
108 Wilmot Road
Deerfield, IL 60617

**Food and Nutrition Information and
    Educational Materials Center**
National Agricultural Library
U.S. Department of Agriculture
Beltsville, MD 20705

Foodservice and Packaging Institute
1025 Connecticut Avenue N.W., Suite 513
Washington, DC 20036
(202) 822-6420

Indiana University
Audiovisual Center
Bloomington, IN 47401
(812) 855-2853

International Film Bureau Inc.
332 South Michigan Avenue
Chicago, IL 60604

Prentice Hall
One Lake Street
Upper Saddle River, NJ 07458

**State Training Branch, DFSR, EDRO Food
    and Drug Administration (CTF)**
Room 8002, Federal Office Building
550 Main Street
Cincinnati, OH 45202

**U.S. Department of Health and Human
    Services**
Public Health Service
Food and Drug Administration
Retail Food Protection Branch
Washington, DC 20201

Appendix B
Commonly Used Terms

Abrasive cleanser

A cleaning compound containing finely ground minerals that is used to scour sinks and heavily soiled areas. Can scratch surfaces and should be used with care.

Acid

A substance that has a pH of less than 7.0.

Acid cleaner

A cleaner used to dissolve heavier deposits of lime, rust stains, and tarnish on equipment and utensils.

Air-dry

A method used to dry equipment and utensils in room air after they have been cleaned, washed, rinsed, and sanitized. Drying cloths are not used.

Air gap

An unobstructed, open, vertical space between a supply of potable water and any possible source of contamination. It is a device used as a preventive measure against backflow.

Alkaline

A substance that has a pH of more than 7.0.

Backflow

The flow of contaminants from unapproved water sources into the supply of potable water.

Back siphonage

A form of backflow that can occur when the pressure in the potable water supply drops below the pressure of the contaminated water supply.

Bacteria

Single-celled microorganisms that require food, moisture, and warmth to reproduce. Some bacteria can cause foodborne infection and intoxication.

Biological contamination

Occurs when microorganisms or toxins that can cause foodborne illness get into food.

Botulism

Type of food intoxication caused by *C. botulinum*. It will develop only without air and occurs in inadequately processed foods, such as meats, many kinds of vegetables, and smoked products.

Carrier

A person who does not show symptoms of a disease but is potentially able to spread the disease to others because a microorganism remains in the person's system.

Chemical contamination

May be caused by chemicals added purposely during processing of food or by accident during any stage of food production. Materials present in the food preparation area, such as pesticides and cleaning compounds, can be put into the food by accident.

Chemical sanitizer

A product used on equipment and utensils after washing and rinsing to reduce the number of disease-causing microorganisms to safe levels.

Clean

Free of visible soil but not necessarily sanitized. A surface must be clean before it can be sanitized.

Cleaning compound

A product used to loosen soil and dirt. Examples are soaps, detergents, acid cleaners, and abrasive cleansers.

Clostridium botulinum

A bacterium that grows without air in improperly processed food and causes the disease called botulism.

Clostridium perfringens

A common bacterium found in the intestinal tracts of humans and animals, as well as in soil, water, and dust. It is often spread by poor employee hygiene and unsafe food handling methods.

Contamination

The presence of harmful substances in food that can cause injury or illness to a person who eats or tastes it.

Control point

Any single step of the receiving, storage, preparation, holding, and serving process at which contamination or alteration of a product could occur.

Corrosion-resistant material   A material that maintains its original surface characteristics under continuous use in food service with normal use of cleaning compounds and sanitizing solutions.

Critical control point   That part of a process where a hazard may be detected and/or eliminated by the action taken at that time.

Cross-connection   A physical link between the potable water supply and a nonpotable or questionable water supply.

Cross-contamination   The transfer of harmful substances from one food to another food either by employee handling or by improperly cleaned and sanitized equipment.

Crustacean   Any of a class of arthropods, including shrimp, crab, and lobster.

Danger zone   The temperature range between 41 and 140°F.

Detergent   A cleaning agent that contains surfactants used with water to break down dirt and make it easier to remove.

Direct physical contamination   Occurs when nonfood objects (hair, glass, pieces from broken equipment) find their way into food as a result of faulty handling.

Easily cleanable   Surfaces that are easy to reach and of such material or finish, so that dirt, soil, and residue may be removed effectively by normal cleaning methods.

Edible   Fit to be eaten.

Employee   Any person working in or for a food service establishment who engages in food preparation or service.

Equipment   All stoves, ranges, hoods, meatblocks, tables, counters, cabinets, refrigerators, freezers, sinks, dishwashing machines, steam tables, and similar items, other than utensils, used in the operation of a food service establishment.

Escherichia coli   A microorganism that always resides in the human intestine and is passed on in feces. The presence of this bacterium in milk or food products is an indication, of contamination, which can cause foodborne illness.

FIFO   First in, first out: the practice of using older food items before newer ones.

First aid   Emergency treatment for injuries and accidents.

Food   Any raw, cooked, or processed edible substance, including ice and beverages, that is used or intended for use in whole or in part for human use.

Food additive   A chemical that preserves foods or improve their flavor. Some, such as sulfites, may have harmful effects on people.

Foodborne illness   Sickness that occurs when contaminated food is eaten.

Food contact surface   The parts of equipment and utensils into which food comes in contact during normal use.

Food establishment   Any place where food is sold or prepared and intended for individual portion service, other than a private home.

Food infection   Caused by harmful live germs or microorganisms that are present in food when consumed.

Food intoxication   Illness caused by food containing the toxins produced by harmful microorganisms.

Food poisoning   A term used to describe illness caused by eating contaminated food.

Fungi   Includes both molds and yeasts; among the most adaptable of all microorganisms, growing readily on all types of food, in moist or dry environments, at any temperature.

Garbage Solid waste generated on the food establishment premises and not disposed of through the sewage disposal system. This term is usually applied to food waste and is a part of the solid waste being discarded.

Germ A general term for a microorganism, including bacteria and viruses.

HACCP The Hazard Analysis Critical Control Point system is a process for monitoring and evaluation of food preparation. By using this system, which is now accepted within the food industry, the risk of contamination and foodborne illness is lowered.

Hazard analysis A classification of food risk factors commonly used as part of the HACCP process.

Hepatitis A A highly contagious virus affecting the liver. It is usually spread by infected food service employees or contaminated shellfish. It is more likely to be transmitted through unheated food items and by items frequently handled during final stages of food preparation, such as salads and sandwiches.

Hermetically sealed container A container sealed by heat and designed to be secure against the entry of microorganisms to maintain the integrity of the contents after processing.

Holding equipment Equipment such as steam trays or tables, steam kettles, heat lamps, and insulated food transport carriers, used to maintain foods at proper temperatures.

Host The organism from which a parasite obtains nourishment.

Hygiene Practices necessary for establishing and maintaining good health and preventing the spread of illness.

Infection An invasion of the body by microorganisms that can multiply and cause a local inflammation, such as a boil, or a general illness such as influenza, food poisoning, or pneumonia.

Infestation   To be overrun by large numbers of harmful parasites, insects, or rodents.

Listeria   A bacterium found in the soil that can contaminate food and cause the foodborne illness called listeriosis.

Manager   The person at a food service establishment who supervises employees responsible for the storage, preparation, display, and service of food to the public.

Meat   Food intended for human consumption that is derived in whole or in part from any portion of cattle, sheep, swine, fowl, fish, shellfish, wild game, or goat.

Microbe   A term used to describe microorganisms.

Microorganism   Tiny life-form, including bacteria and viruses, that can only be seen through a microscope.

Mobile equipment   Small equipment or equipment mounted on casters that one person can easily move.

Mold   Various types of fungi, with a powdery, "furry" appearance, that will grow on most foods in almost any type of environment.

Monitoring procedure   A defined method of checking foods during receiving, storage, preparation, holding, or serving.

Non-food contact surface   An exposed surface of equipment other than food contact surface.

Parasite   Organism that nourishes itself by attaching to other organisms; commonly found in hogs, fish, and contaminated water.

Pasteurization   A process of heating foods to a certain temperature for a specific amount of time to kill bacteria.

Perishable food   Any food that is subject to quick decay or spoilage unless kept in a certain condition (cold, hot, canned, preserved).

Pest control	Repelling or killing harmful insects, birds, and rodents that could contaminate food and food contact surfaces in the food service establishment.
Pesticide	A chemical product used to control insects and rodents.
pH	A measure of the acid or alkaline content of a solution; pH 7.0 is neutral, below 7.0 is acidic, and 7.1 to 14.0 is alkaline.
Poisonous substance	A substance is capable of causing illness or even death when consumed.
Potable water	Water that is safe for drinking.
Potentially hazardous food	Any perishable food that consists in whole or in part of milk or milk products, eggs, meat, poultry, fish, shellfish, crustacea, boiled or steamed potatoes, cooked rice, and refried beans and capable of supporting the rapid growth of harmful microorganisms.
Quaternary ammonium	A chemical sanitizing compound that is relatively safe for skin contact and is generally noncorrosive. It is effective in both acid and alkaline solutions. Also called a *quat*.
Reconstitute	To combine a dehydrated food with water or other liquids to bring it back to its original state: for example, adding water to powdered milk to re-create milk.
Safe temperature	A temperature of 41°F or below, or 140°F or above, used to store potentially hazardous foods. Frozen foods must be kept at or below 0°F.
Salmonella	The bacterium that causes salmonellosis if allowed to grow in food.
Salmonellosis	A food infection caused by bacteria in the intestines of humans and animals; generally found in poultry, red meats, shellfish, eggs, custards, and mixed salads.
Sanitary	Clean and free of harmful organisms.

Sanitize   The final step after washing and rinsing of equipment and utensils. This process reduces bacteria on food contact surfaces to a safe level.

Sanitizing compound   A chemical product, such as chlorine, iodine, and quaternary ammonium, used to reduce the number of bacteria on food contact surfaces to safe levels.

Sealed surface   A surface that is free of cracks and other openings that would permit the entry or passage of moisture and pests.

Sewage   Liquid waste from all sinks, toilets, grinders, floor washing, and hand-washing facilities.

Shelf life   The recommended time that a food item may be stored before it should be used.

Shellfish   Oysters, clams, and mussels.

Single-service article   A plastic utensil, paper napkin, container, lid, placemat, straw, or toothpick designed to be used by one person, one time, and then discarded.

Sneeze guard   A clear, solid barrier that partially covers food in self-service areas to keep customers from coughing, sneezing, or projecting droplets of saliva directly on the food.

Spoilage   Natural decay of foods, which can be increased when they are held at temperatures too hot or cold, or too dry or wet, depending on the product.

Spore   A bacterium that has formed thick walls to resist heat and lack of moisture.

Staphylococcal intoxication   Food poisoning caused by the toxins excreted by tiny microorganisms that live in and on the human body. They grow fast in moist foods high in protein, and are commonly spread by infected workers, poor hygiene, and improper holding and storing of foods.

Staphylococcus

A microorganism commonly found in the nose, throat, skin, and especially in infected cuts, pimples, or boils of humans.

Stationary equipment

Equipment in a food service establishment that is permanently fastened to the floor, table, or countertop. Equipment that cannot be moved.

Storage

A condition of proper packaging of foods, control of temperature and humidity, and provision of a sanitary environment in order to keep food items safe for a period of time before they are used.

Sulfite

A preservative used to maintain the freshness and color of fresh fruits and vegetables. Their use is subject to state regulations.

Surfactant

A chemical agent in a detergent that reduces surface tension, allowing the detergent to penetrate and soak dirt loose.

Tableware

Multiuse eating and drinking utensils, including flatware, plates, glasses, and cups.

Test kit

A device that accurately measures the concentration of sanitizing solutions to ensure that they are at appropriate and safe levels.

Thermometer

A device that indicates temperature.

Toxic

Poisonous.

Toxin

A poisonous substance of plant or animal origin.

Trichinosis

Caused by parasites usually found in pork. These parasites can be effectively destroyed by proper cooking temperatures.

Utensil

A pot, pan, ladle, food container, or any other implement that is used in the preparation, storage, transportation, or serving of food.

Ventilation   Air circulation that removes smoke, odors, moisture, and grease-laden vapors from a room and replaces them with fresh air.

Virus   A microorganism that does not multiply in foods, but can be transmitted to food by infected food workers and then to those who eat the food. Poor personal hygiene often contributes to the spread of a virus to foods.

Yeast   A type of fungus that is not known to cause illness when present in foods, but can cause damage to food products and will change their taste.

Appendix C
Sample Test

1. Potentially hazardous foods that are to be served hot must be held at a temperature of

    a. 120°F or above.

    b. 130°F or above.

    c. 140°F or above.

    d. 150°F or above.

2. Frozen foods should be stored at, or below,

    a. 10°F.

    b. 0°F.

    c. 32°F.

    d. 5°F.

3. The proper method for manual dishwashing in a three-compartment sink is

    a. wash, sanitize, rinse, and air dry.

    b. wash, sanitize, and air dry.

    c. wash, rinse, sanitize, and air dry.

    d. wash, rinse, sanitize, and towel dry.

4. Shellfish offered for sale in a food establishment must

    a. come from a certified packer.

    b. be frozen.

    c. be washed before being cooked.

    d. be removed from the original container.

5. Slicing machines must be cleaned

    a. after each use.

    b. twice a week.

    c. only once each morning before use.

    d. at the shift change.

6. Which of the following is the improper way to thaw food?

    a. Under cold running water

    b. Straight from the freezer to the grill

    c. On a clean surface at room temperature

    d. In a microwave oven

7. One of the most important hygienic practices a food worker can develop is

    a. promptness in reporting to work.

    b. to cover the mouth with hand when coughing.

    c. to wash hands thoroughly and often.

    d. to wipe hands on apron before handling food.

8. *Staphylococcus* multiplies best in

    a. protein foods.

    b. acidic foods.

    c. high-sugar foods.

    d. water.

9. After chemically sanitizing, glasses should be

    a. rinsed with plain water.

    b. wiped with a towel.

    c. air-dried.

    d. stacked with bottoms down.

10. Pork products must be heated to a minimum internal temperature of

    a.   165°F.

    b.   180°F.

    c.   150°F.

    d.   140°F.

11. Pork products that are not cooked adequately may transmit the disease called

    a.   trichinosis.

    b.   scabies.

    c.   impetigo.

    d.   botulism.

12. Cooked or prepared foods that are to be refrigerated before serving should be stored

    a.   above raw foods.

    b.   below raw foods.

    c.   either above or below since contamination cannot occur.

    d.   either above or below if they are covered.

Answers: 1 - c; 2 - b; 3 - c; 4 - a; 5 - a; 6 - c; 7 - c; 8 - a; 9 - c; 10 - c; 11 - a; 12 - a

Appendix D
Sources

Association of Food and Drug Officials and U.S. Department of Health and Human Services (1982). *Retail food store sanitation code.* Washington, DC: Association of Food and Drug Officials and the Food and Drug Administration.

Benenson, A.S. (Ed.) (1990). *Control of communicable diseases in man* (15th ed.). Washington, DC: American Public Health Association.

Bryan, F.L. (1981). Hazard analysis of foodservice operations. *Food Technology, 35(2)*, 78–87.

Bryan, F.L. (1982). *Diseases transmitted by foods: A classification and summary* (2nd ed.). Atlanta, GA: U.S. Department of Health and Human Services, Public Health Service, Centers for Disease Control.

Bryan, F.L. (1982). Microbiological hazards of feeding systems. In *Microbiological safety of foods in feeding systems.* ABMPS Report 125. Washington, DC: National Research Council, National Academy Press.

Bryan, F.L. (1988). Factors that contribute to outbreaks of foodborne disease. *Journal of Food Protection, 41,* 816–827.

Bryan, F.L. (1988). Risk associated with vehicles of foodborne pathogens and toxins. *Journal of Food Protection, 51,* 498–508.

Bryan, F.L. (1988). Risk of practices, procedures and processes that lead to outbreaks of foodborne disease. *Journal of Food Protection, 51,* 663–673.

Center for Food Safety and Applied Nutrition (1986). Interpretation: Potentially hazardous foods. *Retail Food Protection Program Information Manual.* Washington, DC: FDA Center for Food Safety and Applied Nutrition.

Centers for Disease Control (1988). *Foodborne disease control.* Self-study course 3016-G. Atlanta, GA: U.S. Department of Health and Human Services, Public Health Service, Centers for Disease Control.

Chemetka Community College/ Marion County Health Department (1989). *Sanitation manual and food handler's guide.* Marion County, OR: Chemetka Community College/ Marion County Health Department.

Educational Foundation of the National Restaurant Association (1992). *Applied food service sanitation (4th ed.).* New York: Wiley.

Feldman, E.B. (1984). *Programmed cleaning guide for the environmental sanitarian.* New York: Soap and Detergent Association.

Food and Drug Administration (1976). *Food service sanitation manual.* Washington, DC: U.S. Department of Health, Education, and Welfare; Public Health Service; Food and Drug Administration.

Food and Drug Administration (1976). *Manual de higiene para el servicio de alimentos* [Food service sanitation manual]. Washington, DC: U.S. Department of Health, Education, and Welfare; Public Health Service; Food and Drug Administration.

Food and Drug Administration (1985). *PMO: Grade A pasteurized milk ordinance.* Washington, DC: U.S. Department of Health and Human Services, Public Health Service, Food and Drug Administration.

Food and Drug Administration (1988). *Food protection unicode.* Washington, DC: Department of Health and Human Services, Public Health Service, Food and Drug Administration.

Food and Drug Administration (1988). *National shellfish sanitation program manual of operations, part I: Sanitation of shellfish growing areas.* Washington, DC; U.S. Department of Health and Human Services; Public Health Service; Food and Drug Administration.

Food and Drug Administration (1988). *National shellfish sanitation program manual of operations, part II: Sanitation of the harvesting, processing and distribution of shellfish.* Washington, DC: U.S. Department of Health and Human Services, Public Health Service, Food and Drug Administration.

Food and Drug Administration (1991, June 21). *Memorandum on acceptable use of QAC sanitizers.* Washington, DC: U.S. Department of Health and Human Services, Public Health Service, Food and Drug Administration.

Food and Drug Administration. (1993). *Food Code, 1993 Recommendations of the United States Public Health Service Food and Drug Administration.* Washington, DC: U.S. Department of Health and Human Services, Public Health Service, Food and Drug Administration.

Food and Drug Administration. (1995). *Food Code, 1995 Recommendations of the United States Public Health Service Food and Drug Administration.* Washington, DC: U.S. Department of Health and Human Services, Public Health Service, Food and Drug Administration.

Food Marketing Institute (1981). *Management of uniform sanitation training and certification.* Washington, DC: Food Marketing Institute.

Food Marketing Institute (1989). *A program to ensure food safety in the supermarket: The Hazard Analysis Critical Control Point system.* Washington, DC: Scientific and Technical Services Department, Food Marketing Institute.

Harrington, R.E. (1986, April). How to protect your restaurant against foodborne illness: A new approach to sanitation inspection. *NRA News,* 33–34.

Harrington, R.E. (1986, May). Preventing bacterial growth. *NRA News,* 34–36.

Harrington, R.E. (1986, June/July). Characteristics of major foodborne diseases. *NRA News,* 32–34.

Harrington, R.E. (1986, August). How to implement a SAFE program. *NRA News,* 31–33.

Hecht, A. (1991, January/February). The unwelcome dinner guest: Preventing foodborne illness. DHHS Publication (FDA) 91-2244. Reprinted from *FDA Consumer Magazine.*

International Association of Milk, Food and Environmental Sanitarians (1987). *Procedures to investigate foodborne illness* (4th ed.). Ames, IA: IAMFES.

International Association of Milk, Food and Environmental Sanitarians (1991). *Procedures to implement the Hazard Analysis Critical Control Point system.* Ames, IA: IAMFES.

Kinzel, B. (1991, August). Breaking the salmonella/chicken connection: Irradiation is approved for poultry processing. *Dairy, Food and Environmental Sanitation,* 431–432.

Longree, K. and Armbruster, G. (1987). *Quantity food sanitation* (4th ed.). New York: Wiley.

Marriott, Norman G., Department of Food Science and Technology, Virginia Polytechnic Institute (1989). *Principles of food sanitation* (2nd ed.). New York; Van Nostrand Reinhold.

National Fisheries Institute. (1992, September). Seafood safety: How is seafood inspected? *Dairy, Food and Environmental Sanitation,* 619–620.

New York State Department of Health, Office of Public Health, Center for Environmental Health (1991). *Environmental health manual.* Item CSFP 853, with generic HACCP charts. Albany, NY: New York State Department of Health, Office of Public Health.

Reed, G.H., Jr. (1992, August). Sanitation in food service establishments. *Dairy, Food and Environmental Sanitation,* 566–567.

Reed, G.H., Jr. (1992, October). Tests for food spoilage. *Dairy, Food and Environmental Sanitation,* 666–667.

Robbins, M.A. (1992). Evolution and maturation of HACCP. *Environmental Health Review, The Journal of Canadian Institute of Public Health Inspectors, 36* (4), 94–95.

Snyder, O.P., Jr. (1992, July). HACCP, an industry food safety self control program, part VII: Control of surface microorganisms and bioforms. *Dairy, Food and Environmental Sanitation,* 525–529.

Snyder, O.P., Jr. (1992, August). HACCP, an industry food safety self control program, part VIII: Basic considerations in environment, facilities, and equipment control. *Dairy, Food and Environmental Sanitation,* 574–577.

Snyder, O.P., Jr. (1992, October). HACCP, an industry food safety self control program, part X: Derived overall microbiological standards for chilled food processes. *Dairy, Food and Environmental Sanitation,* 687–688.

Snyder, O.P., Jr. (1992, November). HACCP, an industry food safety self control program, part XI: Food system supplier quality assurance (QA) HACCP certification criteria. *Dairy, Food and Environmental Sanitation,* 756–758.

Snyder, O.P., Jr. (1992, December). HACCP, an industry food safety self control program, part XII: Food processes and controls. *Dairy, Food and Environmental Sanitation,* 820–823.

U.S. Department of Agriculture (1988). *The safe food book: Your kitchen guide.* Home and Garden Bulletin, 241. Washington, DC: U.S. Department of Agriculture, Food Safety and Inspection Service.

U.S. Department of Agriculture (1989). *A margin of safety: The HACCP approach to food safety education.* Washington, DC: U.S. Department of Agriculture, Food Safety and Inspection Service.

U.S. Department of Agriculture (1989, May). *FSIS facts: Preventable foodborne illness.* FSIS-34. Washington, DC: U.S. Department of Agriculture, Food Safety and Inspection Service.

Winston, E.W. (1991, August). Food service sanitation guidelines to avoid food poisoning outbreaks. *Dairy, Food and Environmental Sanitation,* 430.

Appendix E
Chapter Review Answers

Chapter 1

1.   To provide safe food.

2.   A.   Identifying hazards to the public health.

     B.   Developing or implementing specific policies, procedures, or standards.

     C.   Coordinating training, supervising, or directing food preparation activities.

     D.   Conducting in-house self-inspections.

3.   A.   Receiving

     B.   Storing

     C.   Thawing

     D.   Cooking

     E.   Holding/displaying

     F.   Serving

     G.   Cooling

     H.   Reheating

     I.   Transporting

Chapter 2

1.   An infection or intoxication caused by contaminated food.

2.   A.   Biological

     B.   Chemical

     C.   Physical

3.   From food to food (raw and cooked) or from unclean surface to food, and vice versa.

4. A food that is neutral or nearly neutral on the pH scale, has enough water and nutrient, and is kept between 70 and 140°F.

5. A. Moisture

   B. Nutrients

   C. Warm temperature

   D. pH level that is slightly acid, neutral, or slightly alkaline

6. A

7. C

8. Send the employee home.

9. Unclean hands are a main cause of foodborne illness. Human skin is a good carrier of bacteria. Hands pass bacteria from contaminated foods and surfaces to otherwise safe food.

Chapter 3

1. Hazard Analysis of Critical Control Points.

2. A. Improper cooling

   B. Temperature danger zone

   C. Personal hygiene of employees

   D. Insufficient temperature in reheating

   E. Improper hot-holding

   F. Cross-contamination

3. One of several steps or hazards in the food preparation process when close attention needs to be paid to proper procedure, to prevent contamination.

Chapter 4

1. No

2. A. Proper temperatures

   B. Packaging

      C.   Dirt

      D.   Odors

      E.   Pest evidence

      F.   Truck conditions

      G.   Proper stamps on meats and poultry products

3.   A.   0°F or less

      B.   41°F or less

4.   First in, first out: To rotate food items so that the older merchandise will be used first.

5.   On the lowest level, so that drippings will not fall on other foods.

6.   C

7.   B

8.   D

9.   C

Chapter 5

1.   Usually from 41 to 140°F, but it may be slightly different in your jurisdiction.

2.   A.   In a refrigerator

      B.   As part of the cooking process

      C.   Under cold, running, potable water

      D.   In a microwave oven, as part of the cooking process

3.   With a metal-stemmed thermometer, testing several different parts.

4.   A.   165°F

      B.   150°F (170°F in microwave)

      C.   130°F

5.   A.   Reheated to 165°F

      B.   Serve at 140°F

6.   Ice-water bath; special refrigerator

Chapter 6

1.   4 inches

2.   A.   Proximity to food handling areas

      B.   Cleaning procedures

      C.   Away from high-traffic area

      D.   Away from garbage area

3.   Six inches

4.   In several areas, especially in warmest areas

Chapter 7

1.   Sanitizing

2.   Scrape; wash; rinse; sanitize; air dry.

3.   A.   100 to 120°F

      B.   140 to 160°F

      C.   180 to 200°F

4.   A.   Hot water at 170°F, 30-second dip

      B.   Chemical: iodine (12.5 ppm) at 75°F/60-second dip; chlorine (50 ppm) at 75°F/60-
            second dip; quats (200 ppm) at 75°F/60-second dip.

5.   With a test kit.

6.   In a sanitizing solution.

7.   Because pests carry and transmit bacteria.

8.   A, B, and D are correct.

Chapter 8

1.   Only in dining areas.

2.   Poor lighting makes it harder to see dirt.

3.   Water that is safe to drink and comes from an approved water supply.

4.   A.   Air-conditioning systems

      B.   Fire prevention

5.   Air gap

6.   As sewage into the sewer system.

7.   After each garbage pickup.

Chapter 9

1.   A.   1.   Keep the place clean and orderly.

            2.   Use slip-resistant floors and shoes.

            3.   Provide adequate lighting.

      B.   1.   Handle hot pots and kettles carefully.

            2.   Keep the place orderly and free of grease.

            3.   Keep flammable materials away from heat.

      C.   1.   Use cutlery carefully.

            2.   Keep cutlery in safe places.

            3.   Use proper guards on machines.

D. 1. Keep gas appliances in good repair to prevent leaks.

2. Keep burnable materials away from anything that leaks.

3. Keep all electrical outlets and equipment in good repair.

2. At all workstations but not in a food preparation area.

3. Get professional medical help—call 911.

4. A. Wood and paper   Class A   triangle—green

     B. Liquids and grease   Class B   square—red

     C. Electrical equipment   Class C   circle—blue

Chapter 10

1. A. Knowledge of the procedures

     B. Motivation to want to do the right thing

     C. Workplace with food policies and procedures

2. To divide a job into small tasks or steps.

3. To guarantee consistency and quality in the procedure, and so employees know what is expected of them.

Chapter 11

1. A. Food and Drug Administration

     B. U.S. Department of Agriculture

     C. Centers for Disease Control

     D. Environmental Protection Agency

     E. Occupational Safety and Health Act

2. To be ready at any time for an official inspection, and to guarantee the production of safe food.

Appendix F
Sample Forms

The following sample forms supplied with this Reference Manual include:

- Food Service Managers/Supervisor Job Description/Evaluation

- Hazard Analysis Critical Control Point Flowchart Worksheet

- Hazard Analysis Critical Control Point Monitor Worksheet

- Hazard Analysis Critical Control Point Monitoring Procedure Report

Food Service Manager/Supervisor
Job Description/Evaluation

Name:	Position:

Date Hired:

Date of Review:

The manager/supervisor must be able to demonstrate the skills and abilities needed to perform management functions. To determine the potential for foodborne illness, the manager must be able to accomplish the following objectives. **Place an "S" for satisfactory or "U" for unsatisfactory performance.**

Accomplishments	Grade
Performs operational assessments of menus and recipes to determine if the food can be produced safely.	
Recognizes standards, policies, and procedures needed to ensure service of safe food.	
Manages personnel.	
a. Selection (hiring, firing, placement)	
b. Trains employees	
c. Supervises	
d. Evaluates	
Implements self-inspection or audit programs.	
Revises policies and procedures as indicated from evaluations.	
Keeps operational records.	
Keeps crisis management plans up-to-date and operational.	
Directs the process flow using principles of sanitation, time/temperature management, employee health and hygiene, and HACCP.	
Identifies approved sources for food and supplies.	
Supervises a receiving program which minimizes the risk of accepting contaminated food.	
Supervises storage procedures.	
a. Enforces the use of FIFO	
b. Monitors temperatures in storage areas	
c. Uses correct equipment	
d. Moves stock to storage immediately	
Supervises preparation procedures applying the principles of sanitation and HACCP.	
Supervises holding, service, and display procedures applying the principles of sanitation and HACCP.	

5/7/92

Accomplishments	Grade
Supervises cooling and post preparation storage procedures applying the principles of sanitation and HACCP.	
Supervises food transportation applying the principles of sanitation and HACCP.	
Complies with federal, state, and local regulations.	
Manages maintenance and repairs of the facility.	
The manager/supervisor demonstrates mastery of the knowledge needed to understand and use good sanitary practices. This includes the ability to identify:	
Terms associated with foodborne illness.	
Microorganisms and toxins that can contaminate food.	
Methods used to minimize the risk of foodborne illness.	
Chemical and physical contaminations that cause associated illnesses.	
Major contributing factors to the increase of foodborne illness.	
Time/temperature factors which can lead to foodborne illness during the following stages:	
Purchasing	
Receiving	
Storing	
Thawing	
Cooking	
Holding/displaying	
Serving	
Cooling	
Storing (post production)	
Reheating	
Transporting	
Uses thermometers to monitor food safely.	
Employee practices which could contaminate food.	
Principles of cleaning and sanitizing in food service establishments.	
Problems and potential solutions associated with facility, equipment, and layout.	

Comments:

Employee's Signature:
Evaluator's Signature:
Date Signed:

Hazard Analysis Critical Control Point
Flowchart Worksheet

Date:	Time Started:
Product:	Time Ended:

Ingredients:

STEPS	PROBLEM/HAZARD	CCP	CONTROL/SOLUTION
	_____	_____	_____
	_____	_____	_____
	_____	_____	_____
	_____	_____	_____
	_____	_____	_____
	_____	_____	_____
	_____	_____	_____
	_____	_____	_____
	_____	_____	_____

Comments:

Signature:

1/22/92

Hazard Analysis Critical Control Point
Monitor Worksheet

Product:

Ingredients:

Date: | Time Start: | Time End:

Time	Temperature	Action

Time/Temperature (°F) Chart

200
190
180
170
160
150
140
130
120
110
100
90
80
70
60
50
40
30
20

0 1 2 3 4 5 6 7 8 9 10 11 12 13

Time in Hours

Signature(s) of Observer(s):

_____

_____

1/22/9

NEW YORK STATE DEPARTMENT OF HEALTH
Bureau of Community Sanitation and Food Protection

Hazard Analysis
Critical Control Point Worksheet

Establishment Name_____ Name of Contact Person_____

Address_____ County_____ Zip Code_____

Date: [mo. | day | yr.]   TIME: Start [ ] : [ ] am/pm   End [ ] : [ ] am/pm

Product_____

Ingredients_____
_____

Sources_____
_____

Time	Temp.	Procedure/Observation	Comment/Interpretation

Time/Temperature (°F) Chart

Product Flow Chart

Name of Inspector

INSTRUCTIONS: Inspector may use this form to collect information for completion of the Hazard Analysis Critical Control Point Monitoring Procedure Report.

DOH-2615 (6/89)

NEW YORK STATE DEPARTMENT OF HEALTH
Bureau of Community Sanitation and Food Protection

Hazard AnalysisCritical Control Point Monitoring Procedure Report

COUNTY		DIST.				EST. NO.				MONTH		DAY		YEAR	

THIS FORM CONSISTS OF TWO PAGES AND BOTH MUST BE COMPLETED.

Establishment Name_____Operator's Name_____

Address_____

(T)(C)(V)_____County_____

Food_____.

PROCESS (STEP) CIRCLE CCPs	CRITERIA FOR CONTROL	MONITORING PROCEDURE OR WHAT TO LOOK FOR	ACTIONS TO TAKE WHEN CRITERIA NOT MET
RECEIVING/ STORING	☐ Approved source (inspected) ☐ Shellfish tag ☐ Raw/Cooked/Separated in storage ☐ Refrigerate at less than or equal to 45°F	☐ Shellfish tags available ☐ Shellfish tags complete ☐ Measure food temperature ☐ No raw foods stored above cooked or ready to eat foods	☐ Discard food ☐ Return food ☐ Separate raw and cooked food ☐ Discard cooked food contaminated by raw food ☐ Food temperature: 　More than 45°F more than 　2 hours, discard food 　More than 70°F, discard food
THAWING	☐ Under refrigeration ☐ Under running water less than 70°F ☐ Microwave ☐ Less than 3 lbs., cooked frozen ☐ More than 3 lbs., do not cook until thawed	Observe method Measure food temperature	Food temperature: 　More than or equal to 70°F, discard 　More than 45°F more than 2 hours, discard
PROCESSING PRIOR TO COOKING	Food temperature less than or equal to 45°F	Observe quantity of food at room temperature Observe time food held at room temperature	Food temperature: 　More than 45°F more than 2 hours, discard food 　More than 70°F, discard food
COOKING	Temperature to kill pathogens Food temperature at thickest part more than or equal to _____°F	Measure food temperature at thickest part	Continue cooking until food temperature at thickest part is more than or equal to _____°F
HOT HOLDING	Food temperature at thickest part more than or equal to _____°F	Measure food temperature at thickest part during hot holding every _____ minutes	Food temperature: 140°F - 120°F: 　More than or equal to 2 hours, discard; less than 2 hours, reheat to 165°F and hold at 140°F 120°F - 45°F: 　More than or equal to 2 hours, discard; less than 2 hours, reheat to 165°F and hold at 140°F

Food _____ Establishment Name _____ Date _____

PROCESS (STEP) CIRCLE CCPs	CRITERIA FOR CONTROL	MONITORING PROCEDURE or What To Look For	ACTIONS TO TAKE WHEN CRITERIA NOT MET

COOLING	Food 120°F to 70°F in 2 hours: 70°F to 45°F in 4 additional hours by the following methods: (check all that apply)
	☐ Product depth less than or equal to 4"
	☐ Ice water bath and stirring
	☐ Solid piece less than or equal to 6 lbs.
	☐ Rapid chill refrigeration
	☐ No covers until cold
		Measure temperature during cooling every _____ minutes
		☐ Food depth
		☐ Food iced
		☐ Food stirred
		☐ Food size
		☐ Food placed in rapid chill refrigeration unit
		☐ Food uncovered
			Food temperature:
			120°F - 70°F
			  more than 2 hours, discard food
			70°F - 45°F
			  more than 4 hours, discard food
			45°F or less
			  but cooled too slowly, discard food

PROCESSING SLICING DEBONING MIXING DICING ASSEMBLING SERVING	Prevent contamination by:
	Ill workers not working
	Worker hands not touching ready to eat foods
	Worker hands washed
	Cold potentially hazardous food at temperature less than or equal to 45°F
	Hot potentially hazardous food at temperature more than or equal to 140°F
	Equipment and utensils clean and sanitized
		Observe:
		Workers' health
		Use of gloves, utensils
		Handwashing technique
		Wash & sanitize equipment & utensils
		Use prechilled ingredients for cold foods
		Minimize quantity of food at room temperature
		Measure food temperature
			If yes to following, discard:
			Ill worker is working
			Direct hand contact with ready to eat food observed
			Cold potentially hazardous food: More than 45°F more than or equal to 2 hours, discard; More than 70°F, discard
			Hot potentially hazardous food
			140°F - 120°F
			  More than or equal to 2 hours, discard; less than 2 hours, reheat to 165°F and hold at 140°F
			120°F - 45°F
			  More than or equal to 2 hours, discard; less than 2 hours, reheat to 165°F and hold at 140°F
			If yes to following, discard or reheat to 165°F:
			Raw food contaminated other foods
			Equipment/utensils are contaminated

REHEATING	Food temperature at thickest part more than or equal to 165°F	Measure food temperature during reheating	Food temperature less than 165°F, continue reheating

HOLDING FOOD, HOT/COLD
 	
TRANSPORTING FOOD
	Food temperature
	☐ More than or equal to 140°F at thickest part
	☐ Less than or equal to 45°F at thickest part
		Measure food temperature during holding every _____ minutes	☐ Hot holding potentially hazardous food: 140°F - 120°F
			  More than or equal to 2 hours, discard; less than 2 hours, reheat to 165°F and hold at 140°F
			120°F - 45°F
			  More than or equal to 2 hours, discard; less than 2 hours, reheat to 165°F and hold at 140°F
			
			☐ Cold holding potentially hazardous food temperature: 45°F - 70°F
			  More than or equal to 2 hours, discard; less than 2 hours, serve or refrigerate
			  More than or equal to 70°F, discard

I have read the above food preparation procedures and agree to follow and monitor the critical control points and to take appropriate corrective action when needed. If I want to make any changes, I will notify the Health Department prior to such a change.

Signature of person in charge_____

Signature of inspector_____

Index